Buying

Practical Finances
For
Small Business Owners

Bob Berry

Three Strands Publishing, LLC

Praise for Buying Bacon

"*Buying Bacon* boils down business finances into layman's terms. This material is old hat to an experienced businessperson, but I would have loved to have had this book in my hands 25 years ago." – Matt Timberlake, Executive Vice President of Corporate Development, Vortex Companies, Ted Berry Company

"My husband and I really enjoyed Bob's *Buying Bacon* presentation and it helped move our small family business forward! Bob's humorous delivery and his personal experience validated the strengths we each bring to the table. The timing was right for us and almost immediately we found ourselves engaged in more robust discussion and questioning about current practices. This led to implementation of new strategies in the areas of budgeting and project planning and, just a few months later, we are already reaping the benefits! Thanks Bob!"
-Denise Boothby, Boothby's Orchard and Farm

"*Buying Bacon* is an easy to read, easy to understand book that gives suggestions that are easy to implement. As I was reading the book, I felt like the author was chatting with me over a cup of coffee instead of lecturing me like a college professor."
-Kendall Bliss

"Bob's *Buying Bacon* study is a great way to reinforce the timeless truths of budgeting. His deep knowledge of the subject and wit brings a great freshness to a topic that many of us think might be 'boring.' I have gained a better understanding of true business profitability because of Bob's *Buying Bacon* study."
-Joel Gilbert, Berry Fruit Farm

"In *Buying Bacon,* Bob broke down the HOW and WHY task of budgeting into terms anyone could understand and apply successfully (even this non-detailed, non-number-loving business owner). I applied his tips and steps to our business as soon as I left the workshop and have seen the focus and growth in just a few short months and am excited to continue. As a bonus, Bob delivers this session in an entertaining manner (which can be tough considering the topic)...[*Buying Bacon*] is an amazing tool full of business tips, inspiration and resources which I keep right next to my computer."
-Betsy Mancine, Renovation CrossFit

"Using the insight and strategy I learned from the class, I have been able to restructure my budget and business model to better posture my business for success!"
-Josh Hill, Allied Realty

BUYING BACON
Practical Finances for Small Business Owners

Three Strands Publishing, LLC
PO Box Q
Livermore Falls, Maine 04254

For Lisa-Anne Berry,

my sweetness revealed.

Table of Contents

Preface

Sometimes, I don't understand what people are thinking.

Take, for example, a businessman I knew. He worked his entire adult life building a successful small business. This business of ten employees was stable, profitable even during the Great Recession, and well regarded in the industry.

Then he sold that business to a young man –basically still a kid – who had no idea what to do with it. That businessman took a huge risk. What was he thinking?

The owner was Darryl. The company was Main-Land. That business kid was me. At 38 years of age, I was in charge of my first real business. I was a new small business owner.

When I bought the business, I was a project manager for the company. I could talk with clients. I knew the work of the company. I was friendly with the team. I could make things happen. Operationally, I thought I knew what to do.

I had no idea how to handle the money.

When I signed on the line and bought Main-Land from Darryl, I was in a bit of a daze. When I got home, my wife saw my look and asked me, "How do you feel?"

I answered, "Like I just got married ten more times."

This was not a game. I now had responsibility for not only my own family, but for ten others as well. They were all counting on me to get this right. That yoke settled firm and cut deep into my shoulders.

I quickly discovered business cash flow wasn't a steady stream. Compared to my household, the business cash flow was a fire hose, blasting at high pressure one moment, trickling the next.

To protect my people and financially succeed, I had no choice but to learn and painfully adapt. I changed my behavior with money.

Over the next ten years, I learned some new and old methods of handling the money of a small business. I am an engineer by trade, so I did what all good nerds do. I read some books… just like you are right now. Nerd. I also attended training seminars. And I talked with other business owners as I dared.

I tried some money methods, implementing some and rejecting others. Every owner and every business are different. A great financial system had to work for me.

Eventually, I landed on a method that works, which is included in this book. I still use it to this day. There is also another way for people who are not nerds. That method is also included in this book, though they have no idea right now because only nerds read the preface.

Don't be offended. Only meganerds write prefaces.

In early 2019 I was asked to speak at a local Chamber of Commerce breakfast meeting. I noticed too many businesses failing in a good economic period. Most businesses fail due to money problems. It seemed I should share a little about what I had learned. How should a small business handle their money to minimize the risk of financial failure? I had plenty of material for this short speech.

The speaking engagement went pretty well. About a third in attendance paid little attention because they were just there to eat breakfast and network. Another third had been there and done that. This material was old hat to them. But the last third were fully engaged and took tons of notes. Notes! They actually wrote down what I was saying! Pages of it! I was floored!

I was asked to speak about it again. People new to business are hungry to learn this material. So, apparently, are you.

While financial knowhow is critically important, it's not exactly thrilling. There are other books on handling money, but they naturally tend to be dry and a little stuffy. You know what I learn when I'm bored? Absolutely nothin'. It's my intent to bring this critical information alive for you. It needs to be real. It needs to mean something so you can apply it and grow.

Are you a new business owner? Have you been operating your business for years but don't have anything to show for it? This book aims to teach you how to handle your small business cash flow. If you work hard, sell well, and handle the money instead of it handling you, there will be profit for you to take home. By profit, I mean cold hard cash. A full bank account. Do you know what you can do with profit?

Buy bacon.

Chapter 1: Making Money
The reason you got into business.

"I am not a product of my circumstances. I am a product of my decisions." - Stephen Covey

"Accountants define profit differently than entrepreneurs. They point to a fictitious number at the bottom of an accounting report. Our definition of profit is simple: cash in the bank. Cold. Hard. Cash. For us. At the end of the day, the start of a new day, and every second in between, cash is all that counts. It is the lifeblood of your business. Do you have it or not? If you don't, you're in trouble, and if you do, you are sustained." - Mike Michalowicz

"The question isn't who is going to let me; it's who is going to stop me." - Ayn Rand

One chill March afternoon years ago, I sat in my office working diligently on a proposal for a big project.

I was deeply focused on the proposal for a significant land development project for a new grocery store. Deep focus is normal for an engineer like me, but I was especially motivated. Springtime is a hard time for us financially and March is the worst.

Work piled up in our queue. Clients called, anxious to be first in line for the summer season. Everyone waited for the last bit of snow to melt so our staff could get going in the field. Cabin fever was in full swing. Our outdoor professionals chomped at the bit, just itching to get outside. Occasionally, one of them risked the deep, soft snow, and disappeared until mud season.

Meanwhile, cash was tight. The long winter slowed work orders. Then one large project owner delayed payment because he was cold, went to Florida for a month and sat on a beach! I had a hard time being angry at him because I wanted to *be* him. Our credit line was maxed. Our checking account bounced on empty. A few vendors hadn't been paid. Just enough money came in the door to keep us afloat. We only had to hold out a week or two more until the snow finished melting.

The proposal I was writing could keep us going well into next winter.

Someone knocked on my office door, pulling me painfully out of my deep focus.

"Do you have a minute," my office manager asked. She looked apologetic and a little pale.

I glared at her for a moment, my emotions still battling with the proposal. But with the effort necessary for many engineers, I softened my expression so she would know she wasn't the problem.

"We have a problem," she said, closing the door behind her. "We're out of money and payroll is due tomorrow."

I knew we were low on cash. I knew payroll was going to be due. My office manager warned me this might happen, but I had told her we would figure it out when and if we ran out of money. I told her to have faith, it would be all right. I am an unabashed optimist.

"Well," I said, "can we take more money from the credit line? Wait, no, that's maxed."

She gave me the deadpan stare every boy has feared since primary school.

"How short are we?" I asked.

"Thirty-five hundred," she replied, relieved I was at least asking the right questions.

"Uh oh."

"Yeah."

We discussed what to do. I had no money. I had nothing that would sell in time. Paying staff was a must. No delays. I owed a metric ton of money to the bank, so I was unwilling to go to them for a loan and risk losing their confidence.

So, I drove to that very bank in our small town, said hello to the teller I personally knew, and then took a cash advance on the company credit card to deposit in the checking account.

Awkward.

As I drove back to the office with sweaty fingers gripping the wheel, I thought to myself, "Never again. Never again. Never again. Never again." The mantra held the anxiety at bay and kept me from asking myself, "Why did I go into business and how do I get out?"

Going into Business

Why did you go into business? There are lots of reasons people take the leap.

I know one fellow who inherited a pizza parlor from his dad. That dude hated pizza but loved his dad.

A woman started her own real estate business because she knew no one could do it better. She might be right.

A friend opened a farm store, selling farm fresh products, soups, and baked goods, including a maple-glazed donut with crumbled bacon. He may be the reason I stay fat. He told me he has always been an entrepreneur since childhood. It's in his blood.

Maybe you need flexibility to your work week. Perhaps you always longed to be the master of your own destiny. Or maybe you're that person, the one who needs to work alone because no one can get along with you.

I went into business because I was asked. The owner and founder of Main-Land was ready to sell. He decided I was the guy to buy it, so he asked me. I knew basically nothing about running a business, but I said yes in no small part because I would be making more money.

At some level, every person who has started or bought a small business did so speculating they would make more money. Business ownership is a huge risk. There had better be a reward.

Good news: it's true. Business owners should and typically do make more. We often work harder and longer, sometimes unseen. We stress more, also unseen except by our spouse. We risk more, totally unseen. We do it willingly to help people, to make a positive impact on our world, to leave a legacy of accomplishment, and to be financially rewarded for all that effort, stress, and risk.

So why was I broke?

Was I Really Broke?

So, was I really broke?

My accountant didn't think so. He and his talented staff provided me with reports, figures, and tables of data which said I made money. There was even this profit report thingy that said my company made six figures last year.

"Yeah, but…"

Yeah, but where was the cash? My checking account didn't have six figures, or any figure but emaciation. I hadn't given away that kind of money. Was I robbed? Where did it go?

My accountant is very smart, and I trust him. But when I asked him how this could be, his answer didn't help. He got very technical with some unintelligible financial jargon. Basis apparently has nothing to do with baseball. You can appreciate a nice sports car but not depreciate an ugly car. Goodwill is not a non-profit used clothing store. Apparently, assets must match liabilities, which makes no sense. He finished up this conversation with great enthusiasm while I just sat there, flummoxed.

Being young at the time and full of myself, there was no way I would admit my ignorance. Rob, if you're reading this, I am very sorry. I must be a nightmare client.

I have come to understand that accountants think backward. Perhaps they are trained to be that way. Maybe it's natural and draws them to the trade. Regardless, the way they think is good and absolutely necessary, because they work closely with the United States Internal Revenue Service.

Dear IRS agent reading this. I totally love your agency and I love paying taxes. I love your boss, your contribution to our great nation, and your dog. I trust you have never targeted anyone due to their political or philosophical views. And it's really cold in Maine. For the two days it's warm, we have mosquitos. Big ones. You'll be much happier staying in DC.

My accountant said profit is my company's revenue minus non-taxable business expenses. The taxable expenses, business related or not, are profit. The IRS taxed that as profit. And it was money I had already spent. The reports show me what happened in the past, not what is happening now or preparing me for the future.

Where had the money gone? It had floated away on company events, new hires, debt payments, and company growth in general. I had no budget, so there's no telling where it went for sure.

For anyone thinking ahead, I know your objection. Yes, my company was now more valuable. That's where the money went. But company value isn't going to meet payroll, pay for an opportunity, or fend off Uncle Sam when he comes calling.

Taxes Cause Pain

If your accountant is as good as mine, you'll want to listen to them. Carefully. But don't misunderstand their role.

Your accountant isn't responsible for making sure you make money. Time to buckle up, buttercup. Making you money isn't their job. Making money is *your* job.

An accountant's job is to take an accounting of what you have already done with your money to determine your tax liability. In other words, they will tell you how much you need to pay the government to keep them from taking your business, your home, and your dog. You don't believe IRS agents buy their own dogs, do you?

When Uncle Sam wants his money, he isn't polite about it, spangly suit aside. Failure to pay comes with painful fines. Then he hits you with interest until you pay it off. He has no sense of humor about it.

That said, the IRS isn't evil. In fact, the IRS agents I've met were helpful and friendly. They're just responsible for making sure you pay the taxes required of you by law. Don't blame the IRS for a high tax burden. Blame an entitled voter block and selfish politicians.

Taxes cause pain. So, take them seriously.

It gets worse. You find out about your tax burden immediately after your accountant tells you about all this invisible money you made. That's right. This is how it happens, while sitting across from your accountant.

He smiled and told me, "You made six figures last year! Congrats!"

"No, I didn't. I'm broke. I just used a credit card cash advance to make payroll," I replied.

"That sucks," he said.

"And I have no bacon."

"Sorry. But we really must talk about your tax bill," he redirected. "The good news is you made money. The bad news is now you need to pay your taxes. You'll owe a metric ton."

"Why metric?"

"Because no one really understands it. Softens the blow with misdirection. Anyway, don't worry. You'll have a fortnight to make payment."

"Fortnight?" I was confused.

"Taxes must be mailed in fourteen days. Or we can file for an extension, but you still need to pay in fourteen days or face fines and interest payments."

Losing my cool, I quipped, "Was it this bad in 1773 when all that tea got dumped in Boston Harbor? No wonder we rebelled."

I may have overdramatized this.

To sum up, I had no money. I was paying 26% on a cash advance on the company credit card to make payroll. I had a tax bill of a metric ton due in a fortnight. And I was in debt up to my eyeballs.

Tapping into the Power

This is where I tell you how brilliant I am.

I used machinations of high-order mathematics and creative financing. I used secret engineering calculations that I could tell you about, but then I would be prematurely ostracized from the clandestine group: Northern Engineers Recalculating Dilemmas Systematically. After all that, I reorganized our checkbook, paid off the credit card, smiled as I handed Uncle Sam a check in a standard english amount, and paid off all my debts so I could sleep at night on a full belly of bacon.

Do you like my fantasy land?

What I really did was curl up in a fetal position for a while. My eyes watered a bit. There was snot.

Then I prayed quite a bit. Praying calms me down because I'm tapping directly into the Creator of the universe. If that's not your thing, then I hear yoga on a beach is relaxing. I don't look good in yoga pants. I kept scaring the tourists.

Finally, I went to work. I reviewed our accounts receivable, figured out what was likely to come in, and called a few clients I knew would pay quickly. I reviewed our expenses and made some hard choices on who would have to wait.

And, I stopped paying myself.

Not paying yourself is common in the world of entrepreneurs. Starting your own business isn't for the faint of heart and requires dangerous periods of time when you get no income. Why do you think most start-ups fail so quickly?

I normally pay myself a regular check just like the rest of my staff. Further, the IRS frowns rather seriously at business owners who take disbursements in lieu of payroll. It has something to do with FICA, which is a metric term for the cost of government benefits.

My family relied on those paychecks. We used those paychecks for some crazy things like buying groceries to feed three teenage boys and making mortgage and car payments. Do you have any idea how much three teenage boys will eat in one afternoon?

I was the one that didn't handle my finances. I was the one who didn't think about taxes. I was the one who bought a business and knew next to nothing about how to make it work. The previous owner wasn't at fault. My accountant wasn't at fault. My staff wasn't at fault. It was all on me. When the money ran out, I was the one who didn't get paid.

I didn't take a paycheck for nearly two months. I had no emergency fund. The mortgage didn't get paid. The cars didn't get paid. The utilities didn't get paid. My boys ate everything in sight, even the mystery cans with no labels in the back of the cupboard. My wife's fat cat didn't come out of hiding until summer. I was looking at that critter with bar-b-que on my mind.

In time, clients paid their bills. The snow melted and our crews went into full beast mode. The tax bill was paid, on time. The card was paid off. I started taking a paycheck again.

I spent months digging my way out of that financial hole.

The bank branch manager is also a friend and colleague of mine. Before long I got a call to tell me about something called an operating capital single-payment loan. If you hadn't guessed, I failed to hide anything from them. They're very smart people who just wanted to help.

Stubborn pride and fear of failure are not good bedfellows.

Handling the Money

If you have been in business for more time than it takes to sit through your wife's favorite musical (she says it's more like the last two minutes of a football game) then you know firsthand what this is like. Finances are stressful. It isn't fun. It makes you wonder why you went into business in the first place.

You did it, in part, to make money! Real money, not accountant money. Money to send your kids to college. Money to go on vacation. Money to retire early or start a second career someday. If you're totally nuts, money to buy another business and do it all again. In other words, all the effort, stress, and risk should result in some cold, hard cash.

Great gobs of money are flowing through your business. Cash flow is your money in and money out.

Profit in the form of cash is when more money comes in than goes out.

Wealth is the part of profit you save, invest, and build.

This book is about the *practical handling of your cash flow so there is money to be used to build wealth.*

Do you know what you can do with wealth? You guessed it. Buy bacon!

Bacon Bits

- If you own a business, you do so, in part, to make money.
- A positive net income on an accountant's report is nice, but ultimately you want money in your bank account.
- You need actual money in the bank to pay taxes and financially survive.
- Ensuring financial survival and prosperity takes sacrifice, hard work, and knowledge.

Chapter 2: Tuning the Revenue Machine
What else is needed to make money?

"Momentum rarely occurs after one crazy effort. Momentum builds slowly but relentlessly. Small, repetitive, continuous actions, chained together, build momentous momentum." -Mike Michalowicz, Profit First

"You plus God equals enough." - Zig Ziglar

"Take your work seriously but never take yourself seriously." - Booth Tarkington, American novelist

When I was twelve years old, I wanted to start making money.

My dad and I fixed up a junk lawn mower that my granddad had in the barn on our rural Embden, Maine farm. My granddad never threw anything away and my dad can fix anything. I then posted a sign at the bottom of our quarter-mile driveway which read, "Lawns Mowed - $5," with my phone number.

Before you think I was industrious from a young age, let's put this in perspective. There was no PlayStation or Xbox. There was no Nintendo. There was no internet. Our phone was attached to the wall and we had no idea who was calling when we answered it. My parents worked hard and provided us with a coveted Atari 2600 and exactly two games: Pac-Man and Super-Breakout. Even then, we had screen time limits, though the limitation method was something like: if the sun was shining, the screens were off.

The point isn't that the number of people willing to call me young is getting alarmingly small, though it's painfully true. The point is I had limited distractions which didn't involve splitting wood or hoeing potatoes. Working to make money seemed preferable to working the woodpile.

Five dollars is a deal for a lawn mowing, right? Even then, it was a deal.

Embden Lake is surrounded by summer camps. There were some locals in those camps, but most folks were well to do and from away. The flatlanders I knew were always really nice. This is when I started to learn wealthy people in real life often don't look like wealthy people on television. "The Pond", as we simply called it, was less than a mile away with camps stretching down the east shore for three miles. I was the only kid with a sign out.

Wealthy people don't like to cut grass. It turns out I didn't like to cut grass, either.

To cut the grass, I strapped the gas can to my belt and pushed the heavy lawn mower from one to four miles to get to the right camp. After mowing, I walked back. Ponds are located at the low point of land, so the return trip was uphill. The mower had no power assisted wheels.

Did I mention the mosquitos?

No one then knew I would become an engineer by trade, but it started to show when I built a bracket to tow the mower with my Huffy ten-speed bike.

Despite the price bargain, I only had three clients. I hadn't noticed most of the camps were well shaded by trees. Grass growth was limited. My sign was on a public road, but at the far end of The Pond where few travelled the dirt roads to see it. Many of the camp owners brought children or grandchildren who mowed what little grass there was.

Business wasn't good.

By July, I knew intuitively this wasn't working. I wanted to quit, but my mom wouldn't let me because I had made a commitment that summer. It goes without saying she was right, because my mom is a well-honed character builder.

My dad played accountant and helped with the after-the-fact math.

I charged five dollars a mowing. One camp was nearby, and the customer was demanding about the mowing schedule. The other two were nearly three miles away, but I could group them together.

Two camps at five dollars each was a ten-dollar day.

I paid for my own gas. Each trip I used three gallons, at a combined cost of just under three dollars. If you remember when gas was under a dollar a gallon, you're old, too.

After expenses, I netted about seven dollars. Seven dollars was a good chunk of money to a rural twelve-year-old boy in those days.

One camp had a little lawn that took half an hour to mow. The other camp had a big lawn and took two and a half hours.

It took an hour to get there and two hours to trudge back.

Doing math, I was making $1.17 an hour. Minimum wage at the time was $3.50.

So, I was forced to question. Why did I get into this business, anyway? It just wasn't worth it.

Can you count the mistakes I made?

There Is More to Buying Bacon than Price

This book is about the practical handling of your cash flow so there is money to be used to build wealth. Cash flow is *money in and money out.*

We're not talking much about making cash come in the door. That's up to you. You're probably already good at it. Most of this book deals with the money that's leaving and how to hold onto some of it.

But I would be remiss if I didn't mention a few critical issues to think about for readers either aspiring to go into business or new to business. This chapter takes a brief look at some key business principles from a very high level which helped me bring revenue in the door.

From Idea to Bacon

Every business starts with an idea. I love this, because there is no end to human inventiveness. We were designed to dream, to chase vision, and to create. Entrepreneurs and small business owners do just that every day. This alone gives me hope for America.

Unfortunately, most people stop right there.

"Hey, wouldn't it be great if backpackers could keep rain off their head while hiking?"

"I wish this blanket had sleeves so my arms stay warm while I stuff my face in front of the TV."

"When I cheer for another Patriot's first down, I spill my beer. Maybe I should hang them somehow on my hat."

Then, two years later, you see it on television and yell, "Hey, that was my idea!"

An entrepreneur brings an idea to a concept. They draw plans, write it down, and most importantly, think it through. There is a certain energy to this that makes my inner engineer giggle a little bit.

Once there's a concept, then it's time to make a prototype. This is where it gets real. Do this by yourself or with trusted friends and family, but make sure to have fun! If it isn't fun, it's just more work.

With a functioning prototype to show, proof it to people you trust will give honest feedback. That's not your (s)mother, who says everything you do is fantastic and would you like a cookie with that. Pick trustworthy people with trade experience.

Your product or service is now ready to develop. Design it so you can make it marketable, repeatable, and profitable.

You need to be able to build a business around your product, with systems for obtaining material or parts, manufacturing, warehousing, distribution, and sales, to name just a few of the more obvious systems.

These initial efforts of idea, concept, prototype, proofing, development, and business building seem obvious but are worth stating. Don't get them in the wrong order.

Supply and Price

Way back in civil engineering college at the University of Maine, Orono (Go Black Bears!), I took courses about structures, concrete, hydrology, soils, and poop. Yes, poop. Wastewater Management was a required course for us.

We also were required to take some elective classes. Being a country boy, I had no idea what I should take. I didn't even know what an elective class was. My advising professor suggested economics, because, "There's a lot of math and engineers tend to do well there." So, I took a string of economics courses.

On the first day of economics class in a room of 200 young students, the wild-haired professor with patches on his elbows yelled, "If there's nothing else you need to learn in this class, it's this! Now is the time to pay attention!"

The whole class stirred as fresh notebook pages were readied and pens were poised for wisdom.

The professor ran to the giant chalkboard, tweed blazer flapping behind, and literally crushed the chalk as he drew a graph, wrote, and screamed at the top of his lungs, "Slope = rise over run!"

I swear he was so fervent spittle flew.

There were several of us engineers at the back of the room. We looked at each other incredulously because the formula for slope is something we learned in middle school. You would get a similar look if you told a mechanic cars run on gas or a pig farmer bacon comes from pork bellies. Apparently, the rest of the class was enamored by this mathematical nugget of genius, because they all diligently wrote it down.

We laughed a little. Quietly, because that's what nerds do when they're not alone.

If you aren't a nerd, have no fear. From this point forward, please forget that slope equals rise over run. Besides, there are annoying exceptions to that rule.

Instead, learn what we learned later in class: The Law of Supply and Demand. When a product demand goes up, the supply gets sold and diminishes. If the supply goes up, less was sold so the demand must have gone down. The two are intrinsically linked. Supply down, demand up. Supply up, demand down. It makes sense when you think about it.

After that, remember demand and price are also intrinsically linked. Demand up, price up. Demand down, price down. Think about this as well. It makes perfect sense.

So, before diving into a business, ask yourself if there's already a heavy supply for the product or service you'll provide. If there's already a lot of your product or service, the demand will be low and so will the price. You may not succeed at all if you can't differentiate yourself from the competition.

If you have something unique (low supply) people want (high demand), you will command a high price.

Get the Word Out

When I bought Main-Land, the previous owner spent little to no money on advertisement. He told me, "Word of mouth is the best advertisement."

He was a brilliant man. Nothing is quite as effective as a reference from a trusted friend.

So, for years I did very little advertising and thought even less about marketing or sales efforts. If asked, I couldn't even define those terms adequately.

Then, despite our best work and happy clients, we plateaued. We just stopped growing.

It turns out that word of mouth is powerful but poorly controlled. We aren't there to guide what people say in private. We can't correct misapprehensions or fill in the gaps about our product offering when we aren't there. We cannot control *where or when* that word is spoken.

We still rely on word of mouth. Without a good company reputation, sales are difficult. But now we don't stop there.

Marketing has many definitions, depending on who you ask. A marketing professor could go on for a week of lectures about that topic alone. My marketing skills were learned in the field, so to speak. So, where the bacon hits the griddle, marketing simply means the effort you make to get the word out about you, your company, and the products or services you offer, with hope to positively impact how people think about you.

There are as many ways to do this as there are marketing professors. Here's a small sample.

Social Media

Social media is a great way to get the word out. It's easy to learn, easy to use, and basically free. Best of all, readership is monstrous! More people use social media than read the newspaper. Sorry, but it's true.

We started with Facebook and LinkedIn. We have Twitter and Instagram accounts, but rarely use them. Snapchat what? Our customer base of landowners is typically middle-aged and older. They use Facebook and LinkedIn. Your customers may have different demographics, so pick accordingly.

Just start posting. Post about your product. Post about your people. Post about your culture. Post about your clients, in as far as that is applicable and safe.

If you have company values, and you should, then start posting about them. Let those values show through in what you write.

If you have a sense of humor, use it. People want to be entertained. If you get a reputation for funny posts, your following will skyrocket. More followers means a greater impact for social media marketing. Go visit the Bangor Police Department Facebook page to see social media humor done right. If a police department can get this right, so can you.

Use pictures and videos as much as feasible. People scroll right past text but will stop to see a picture or short video. Be sure to get permissions from picture subjects, especially from clients. We even show posts containing staff to them before publishing so that they can veto anything they find embarrassing. Also, be careful about what is happening in the background. We sometimes take pictures on construction sites. A picture that shows someone's employee in the background without a hardhat will generate an ugly phone call. Ask me how I know.

Once it's been published, ask staff and friends to like and share them. A post liked and shared grows viewership exponentially, which is called "going viral." Likes and shares increase the opportunity for a post to go viral and get on prospective clients' radars.

Trade Shows and Conferences

Introverts, you just cringed.

Trade shows and conferences are loud, chaotic, and expensive. They're full of people, many of whom you won't like.

Need I remind you that people buy products?

We have rarely made a direct sale at a trade show. But I have talked to many people there who later gave us a shot.

Trade shows are like the golfer setting up on the tee. The ball hasn't been hit yet, but the golfer is now ready to take her swing.

People who lean extrovert love trade shows. People who lean introvert do not. Most of us are somewhere in between.

Your enjoyment here isn't the issue. Your absence is.

Most industry trade shows are filled with a relatively small group of vendors who do what you do, also known as your direct competition. If you aren't there, not only are you missing the opportunity to tee up the ball, your competition has unfettered access to the golf course.

Go. Get used to talking to strangers about what you do. Learn to be friendly and make personal connections. Get a bunch of business cards and even call them later. Maybe even take a few to lunch. That's how it works.

Seminars

As land use consultants, we sell a professional service. Our clients require a friendly professional to help them. What better way to show prospective customers you are a friendly professional in your industry than to teach them something about it?

Whatever it is you do, you know more about it than your customers. Look for the opportunities to teach about it. Trade shows usually have some seminar sessions. Consider teaching one. Your local chamber is always looking for a speaker for their meetings. Adult Education is desperate for new teachers. And if you have the space, consider teaching a course in your own shop.

The point here is, if you have something interesting to teach, people will come to listen. When you teach, show them you have the heart of a teacher. Caring is at the heart of every teacher. Caring for your customer will yield repeat customers.

Advertising

"Advertising pays for itself." That's what the man sitting across the table told me. He was selling ad space in a trade magazine. If he was right, then I gave up a lot of potential income. His advertising was expensive.

Advertising on radio, television, internet banners, newspapers, and the like may be just what your product or service needs. Maybe someday I will need to spend gobs of money on advertising. So far, advertising expenses have yielded little measurable results for my company.

Instead, I tend to spend my limited advertising budget on charitable and non-profit events. If I must choose between buying a media ad or sponsoring a charity 5K run, I will choose the run. (Sponsorship, not actually do the running. If I'm running, something's chasing me.) For my sponsoring dollars, Main-Land's logo gets on the runner's t-shirts, noted in event paperwork, and put on signage. We usually get mentioned in the paper as well. The dollars go not to a media outlet but to a worthy charitable cause. Opportunities for this kind of advertising abound. Say yes to a few.

When I get big enough or have another business model that needs traditional advertising, I plan to do both.

Sales

Marketing and advertising aren't the same as sales. Marketing and advertising lead to the opportunity for sales.

Sales is the process of directly convincing a potential customer your product or service is more valuable than their hard-earned cash.

Sales is both a science and an art.

Sales can be scientifically broken down to constituent parts, such as introduction, approach, vetting, presentation, education, mathematics, communications, closure, and follow up. If you're a nerd, learn sales and practice it, because nerds suck at this. It takes practice to get better. Read some books by Zig Ziglar and jump in. Just don't forget the point is to show a customer your product is more valuable than the price. After that, they make the choice. *In any transaction, the power belongs to the buyer.* They have the power to walk away.

Sales is also an art. Some people are charmers with high levels of charisma. Customers buy into their pitch in a short time and with little effort. I'm not one of those, so I can't help you there. But look for that ability in your hires.

The bad news is without sales your company will wither and die. Sales involves people skills. People skills are hard for many of us.

The good news is that people skills are learned the same way as all your other skills: education, practice, and repeat.

Don't fear the sales process. Don't sit back and figure people will come to you through word of mouth. Rather jump in, sell, and have fun! Besides, you really have no choice. Sales skill is a fundamental pre-requisite to successful business growth.

Goals and Strategy

There was once this pub owner who made great beer.

He knew beer. He loved beer. All kinds of beer. IPAs and lagers. Browns, reds and stouts. He never made a bad beer.

His family encouraged him to open a pub because he made such great beer. It seemed like the right thing to do, so he started making lots of beer and rented a space for a taproom. He asked the government for permission. He got a small business loan, bought furniture, and hired a barkeep. With a ribbon cutting, he was open for business.

His beer was great and so was his barkeep. Pretty soon the taproom was full. Beer flowed out and cash flowed in.

He hired a waitress. Then two. Then four. He brought in takeout food. When that was a hit, he opened a small kitchen. Then he expanded it after he doubled the size of the taproom. He even rented the space next door, busted down the wall, and put in sit-down dining. His pub was in the papers. He was a model citizen, a Chamber director, and helped the town by sitting on the planning board. He was liked and respected by many, and a source of inspiration to aspiring entrepreneurs.

The owner was driven. He knew how to make lots of great beer. He knew how to make his customers happy. He knew how to make money.

But he hated the bustle. He hated the calls from vendors. He hated the occasional crazy customer. He hated the gossip among his wait-staff. He caught his barkeep with his fingers in the till.

A chain opened across the street. Soon his customer base was cut in half. His best two waitresses left to work there. The new barkeep growled at too many customers. The pub owner yelled at him for it and wondered why the barkeep couldn't hold his temper. His bank accounts were empty, his loan payments were due, his staff were quitting because he missed payroll last week, and his customers stopped coming. He had no idea how to turn it around.

Finally, in anxiety, depression, and a little bit of rage, the pub owner locked up his doors for the last time. He didn't tell anyone. He didn't call his parents, his staff, or the bank. He just didn't show up the next morning. He was done. The business had failed.

Businesses open and close all the time. In the end, they almost always fail due to money problems.

Money problems are often symptoms of some other failure. In this case, the pub owner failed to plan. He was driven, creative, and customer oriented. He could make money. But he had no plan. If only he had thought to himself, "Where do I want to be with this business in five years?" He would have immediately answered to himself, "I want to make great beer, bottle it, and sell it to restaurants, stores, and bars all over my region."

See? He loved making and selling beer, but he didn't love running a restaurant. So, he failed.

Do you have a plan for success?

The planning process begins with why you want to own a business and ends with the details of making that business awesome. The steps are:

1. Your main reason why
2. Vision statement
3. Mission statement
4. Big hairy audacious goal
5. Goals
6. Strategies
7. Objectives

Step 1: Why. Sit down for a quiet, solitary moment and ask yourself an important question. Why? Why are you doing this? You need that answer to continue. For example, if you run a coffee shop, your why might be your love for your town and your love of mornings.

Step 2: Vision. Your why is tied to your vision. What is your company's vision? What would you like to see your company accomplish? For example, the coffee shop's vision might be to get their town moving every morning.

Step 3: Mission. A vision then directs your mission, as in the common mission statement. A mission statement is the white lines around a football field. It shows you the goal line, which is the direction you should drive. It also shows you the side lines, which are the out of bounds lines. If you stray outside your field of play, you are no longer on mission. For example, the coffee shop's mission might be, "to provide delicious, energizing coffee for our town every morning so they will all get going!" If the opportunity to sell belt buckles comes along, is that on mission?

Step 4: BHAG. A solid mission statement leads to a goal. Where should your company be in five years? Call it your Big Hairy Audacious Goal (Recommended read: *Built to Last* by Jim Collins). Your BHAG will give specificity to your mission. It'll aim your enterprise at the right stars. Make it so, number one.

Maybe your BHAG is to sell 5,000 handbags with bacon print shoulder straps. Maybe your BHAG is to create a prototype holster for snacks on the go and sell 2,000 of them. Maybe your BHAG is to open an all-you-can-eat bacon bar and grow to $1,000,000 annual revenue and 60-inch girth. Your BHAG is up to you.

Step 5: Goals. Now, what shorter goals do you need to reach your BHAG? What things do you need to accomplish this year? This quarter? For example, a goal may be to open your coffee shop in a downtown location by May.

Each goal aims at the BHAG.

Step 6: Strategies. When planning each goal, set one or more strategies needed to accomplish that goal. If your goal is to set up a new product line, then strategies might include brainstorming, market analysis, cost analysis, stakeholder input, and scheduling.

Step 7: Objectives. Finally, each of those strategies could have one or more objectives. For example, the cost analysis strategy from above may have objectives that include determining material cost, transport cost, assembly cost, packaging cost, inventory storage cost, sales cost, and administrative cost.

Does that seem like a lot? For some readers, no. This level of detail is the cat's rump. Go for it and win!

For others, it's just too much. I tend to agree.

At Main-Land, we have vision, mission, and a BHAG. For goals, we do them one at a time. We operate on a quarterly goal period. Every quarter our leadership team gathers for an offsite meeting where there's lots of food. There we do some team building, company values discussion, and set the next quarterly goal. Then, throughout the quarter, we meet for two hours every other week to report on progress toward that goal and collaborate on the goal's strategies and objectives. We assign the goal to one person, each strategy to individuals, and each objective to individuals. Now, not only is the business owner driving the improvements, so is the whole leadership team and key staff in the organization. They have a stake in the outcome and are motivated to meet the goal.

Our quarterly goals have been things like shortening accounts receivables, developing a profit-sharing model, improving team recognition, developing a project win-loss analysis method, figuring out where to spend our marketing dollars, and launching our first branch office.

We tried to do several goals at once but found we failed to meet them. So, now we focus on one singular goal each quarter. At first it seemed impossible to create a winning situation by focusing on only one goal at a time. After years of four successful strategic goals annually, we found real measurable progress and a far better company. It takes time.

We also found that after a couple of years, our BHAG changed. One time, we decided our BHAG was too audacious, so we reset it to make it more attainable. Another time we decided to change direction to accommodate shifts in the market. But there was always a BHAG. We knew where we were heading.

Set your vision, mission, and BHAG. Make it audacious. Then outline some goals, strategies and objective steps that need to be accomplished to meet that BHAG. Do this with some trusted family, friends, or best yet, leaders in your company. Be flexible but be tenacious. Don't drop the ball. Make it a priority. Only then will you be assured you're working toward something great!

Leadership and Team

Which came first, the chicken or the egg?

Which came first, the leader or the team?

While the first is an age-old cliché, the second has a clear answer. The team always comes first for the leader. Always.

About a bazillion books do a great job teaching leadership and team building. Find a few of them, fry up a pound of bacon, and make a day of it. Go to www.main-landdci.com/bobs-booklist for a selection of books I recommend.

When I teach leadership to my rising stars, I like to break it into three parts: power, service, and vision.

Power

Leaders have power.

I've recently learned how much power I really have. A suggestion is not a suggestion but a clear order that must be obeyed. A frown because I'm still struggling with a client's problem will instill fear in entry level staff. An off-hand comment can stir my entire staff into confusion and disorder.

Dr. Henry Cloud, in his great book *Boundaries for Leaders*, says business owners are "ridiculously in charge." Truer words have never been spoken. You are the owner. You make the rules. You can raise employees up to leadership level or cut them from the team with the wave of your hand toward human resources.

Power can be broken down into two types a leader will commonly wield: positional power and persuasion power.

Positional power is power you have due to your positional authority. It's like the dark side of power wielding. It is easy and quick. Do it because I said so. I'm the boss.

Positional power is also lazy. Instead of taking the time to convince a team member so they buy in, you can just make it so. Positional power is cutting. No one learns much from being told what to do. Positional power is frightening. Do it or else. And position power is heady. If you ever like the sight of your staff scampering to work after you growled, you're no longer a leader worth following.

But don't give it away. Positional power is yours because you are the business owner. Keep it, because you are ridiculously in charge. Just don't wield it unless necessary.

Persuasional power is the leader taking the time to talk with the team to convince them of what must be done. The most important part of convincing is the why. Why must it be done? Why is it important? Will this effort meet an objective? Is it an objective worthy of their effort? Will the team like to go in that direction?

Great leaders are personally convinced of the organization's cause. Great leaders use persuasional power to convince their team in lieu of positional power to direct their team. A team convinced of the reasons why will be self-motivated, energetic, and focused on the tasks to get there.

Service

Leaders are servants.

The term "servant leadership" is so ubiquitous that it is nearly cliché. That doesn't make it any less true. Great leaders have a servant's heart.

Leaders serve their team. Service shows caring. People will only follow someone they trust, and only trust someone who cares. This yields team unity and organizational effectiveness.

Leaders serve their mission. They have a cause and are driven to advance it.

Leaders serve their community. Leaders know that a rising tide raises all boats. A strong and thriving community is mutually beneficial and creates economic opportunity for everyone.

Service isn't difficult. Prolonged service is, so make sure to stay focused on service as a priority.

Vision

My friend and pastor Henry Cooper is cool. He looks cool. He dresses cool. Even the way he talks is cool. It seems almost unfair that he is also a pilot. Pilots are icy cool.

Henry was a pilot for a missionary group when he was younger. He flew planes in South America to bring people and supplies to and from missionaries in remote jungle villages in and around Eastern Bolivia. The flying was dangerous. His planes weren't often equipped with GPS back then, so he sometimes used map and compass to navigate while flying. The maps weren't always drawn right. Imagine plotting a course high enough to fly over a mountain only to have to fly around it when you get there.

Getting lost in a plane was a real danger. The jungles, mountains, and rivers were numerous and tended to look similar. He described looking down at the vast forest as seeing "a sea of broccoli." Once, he misidentified a river, was distracted in conversation with the passengers, and inadvertently ignored the compass for a moment. With a sinking feeling in his gut, Henry realized he was lost. The plane was headed the wrong way, the fuel gauge was dropping almost as fast as the sun, and he had moments to correct his path to land his plane safely while he could still see the unlit runway. The alternative was to crash the plane into a mountain or a dark jungle. His life and the lives of his passengers required his vision, deduction, plan formulation, and execution.

As leaders, it is up to us to recognize when we are lost and on the wrong trajectory. We need to have the vision to picture where we are on the destination path, deduce the implications, and formulate the plan to correct the trajectory.

Once Henry did those tasks, he turned the steering yoke and calmly pointed out the beauty of a passing mountain to his enamored passengers. At dusk, the plane safely landed at the jungle runway where he and his passengers were warmly greeted by the villagers. Henry found a quiet spot out of sight to throw up.

Leaders don't have a physical steering yoke on their organization. Leaders need to persuade their people to adjust and execute the plan. Leaders must turn the plane with only their words.

What would it take to turn the plane without touching the controls? The method would be to shift as much weight in the plane to one side as feasible. The pilot would explain the situation to his key passengers and why the weight needs to be shifted. One key passenger has the idea and executes a shifting of cargo to one side. Another will talk to the other passengers about cramming to one side. One guy wants to talk about the survival odds of the inevitable crash. And the last enterprising leader offers to go out on the wing to increase rotation and drag on that side. At first the plane just rocks back and forth. But with buy in and time, the plane starts to turn, slowly at first but faster as more cargo is moved, and a missionary jumps out on the wing to help. Don't try this at home. It's just a metaphor.

A humble leader knows their own plan may not be the best plan. A leader gathers their key people, lays out the vision, and persuades them the vision is worthy. The humble leader may lay out the framework of a plan, or let the group devise a plan together. The humble leader persuades.

Persuasion leads to buy-in. People buy-in when they have a chance to voice their opinion on what they are buying. People buy in after they weigh in. Leaders give their key people the chance to change the plan. Even if the plan is not changed, at least they had the opportunity to try. *Get weigh-in to have buy-in.*

Leaders and their key people execute the plan. Each person persuades their team members that the plan, and their part in it, is the way to win. Some people will hesitate. Some will question. Some will push back. But with time, consistent persuasion, and signs of success building trust, the organization will turn.

What is your why? What is your purpose? Why are you doing what you are doing? Be strong and clear on these answers first so you know what to share and have the energy to keep at it.

You don't want to crash and burn in the jungle.

Is This All Worth It?

Have you ever heard someone say all that leadership stuff is overrated? Some people think a mission statement is a waste of time. Company values should just be stuffed in a desk drawer and best forgotten. Don't even mention a business plan.

There was a time, perhaps, when a businessperson could ignore these things and have some success. That time has passed.

Today's team members rightfully demand more than financial compensation for their efforts. The millennial generation regards purpose and mission more important than salary. Their priorities are, of course, correct. It just took me half a lifetime to figure it out.

You own your company. You are responsible for driving its success. You are also a prime limiter of your company. In his book *The 21 Irrefutable Laws of Leadership*, John C. Maxwell calls it the Leadership Lid.

Don't be the lid. Learn to operate your business according to your mission, inspire your team, and grow your company to make a legacy impact on your family and community.

Bacon Bits

- If you're contemplating a startup, make sure you take the following minimum steps: idea, concept, prototype, proofing, development, and business building.
- Your product should be low in supply and high in demand to command the highest price and profit.
- Market your business to get the word out though social media, trade shows, conferences, and seminars. Advertise to reach your customers. Get good at selling.
- Know why you are in business. Write a mission statement. Have a big hairy audacious goal for your business, with supporting goals, strategies, and objectives.
- Lead your team with persuasional power. Serve your team to build trust. Cast vision to set direction.

Chapter 3: The Money Mood Cycle
Ride the rollercoaster.

"Too many of us are not living our dreams because we are living our fears." - Les Brown

"It does not do to leave a live dragon out of your calculations, if you live near him." — J.R.R. Tolkien

"**E**eeaarmmph," I grunted. It was half a snarl. I was in a bad mood.

"It's due today," Angela said. She was our office manager at the time. She knew what she was about and didn't flinch as she stared me down. She's an executive with us now, as CAO.

"How much is it," I asked.

"Forty-five hundred."

"Eeeaarmmph."

The bill needed to be paid. Unfortunately, we were rather low on cash.

Cash flow is never linear, never smooth. For three weeks, more cash than I had ever seen came through the door. We got caught up on all our bills and bought some equipment. We had a pizza party!

Then for five weeks, someone turned the valve to the right. Cash slowed to a trickle. We fell behind on our bills.

"What do you think we should do," I asked Angela.

"I'm not sure. When I'm CAO, I'll tell you. Right now, this is your decision."

"What's a CAO?"

"Chief Anything Officer. As in, anything you can do I can do better."

"When I can afford that salary, you've got the job."

"So…" she prompted.

"Hold it until tomorrow," I told her. "I've got a good feeling tomorrow will be a great cash day."

The dry spell lasted for another nine days. Then six digits came through the door in one morning.

Figures.

Revenue In

How does your business get paid?

For most companies selling a physical product, you get paid when the product is sold. Oh, you want this package of delicious bacon? That will be $13.95, please.

Some companies have a payment plan. Don't be shocked, but I attend a gym. Yes, I even go. Sometimes. I don't pay for that gym each time I go but rather have a "membership" at the gym, which is nothing more than a monthly payment plan on the cost to rent their equipment. The gym gets paid whether I go or not. Nice.

Some companies have collateral on getting paid. I've envied mechanics in this regard. If you want the keys back to your newly repaired truck, you'll need to pay for the repairs first.

Still others imply threat. I doubt many people consider not paying their lawyer.

For the rest of us, we count on the good will of friendly customers and the threat of work stopping on their project. This means revenue, cash coming in the door, can vary significantly from day to day, month to month.

If you have experienced a few weeks of slow revenue, then you know the fear of running out of money.

Seasonality

Your method of getting paid may be steady, but your industry may not be. Many industries are seasonal.

If you live up north, then you know all about seasonality. We northerners tend to retreat a little when the snow flies. Business slows right after Christmas. We don't really want to go outside in the cold where the air hurts our face. We prefer a fireplace, flannel pajamas, coffee, and a good book instead of snow up to our collarbones.

Imagine selling garden supplies in February. Contractor's know you can't cast concrete when it's twenty below zero.

Realtors can get better deals on some houses when the lawn is green.

Obviously, work doesn't stop but culturally we tend to slow down during the winter months.

Southerners probably face the same thing during the hot season, minus the frostbite. But we don't have snakes that can kill a full-grown man, so I'll take the cold.

Many businesses rely on tourism. What time of year is best for your business depends on why tourists are coming to your region. I know businesses that are busiest during the hunting seasons. Others rely on fishing season, best flying weather, or legislative sessions.

Some parts of year are cash rich. Some are cash poor. Not all industries are sensitive to the season, but many are. Is yours? Why? Knowing the answers will help you avoid financial failure.

Failure Has Eight Legs

The number one fear among people the world over is not death or spiders. It should be spiders. Spiders are gross.

The number one fear among people the world over is the fear of failure. You read that right. People would rather die than fail.

Failure is a blow to our fragile ego. If your ego isn't fragile, it will be with a big enough failure.

Failure is a blow to our self-image and our projected image. Failure shatters how we view ourselves and how we want others to view us.

Failure sets us back on our journey to success. Failure slows us down.

You have heard all sorts of people talk about failure being important to the learning process. We are smarter and stronger due to our failures. Failure creates pain. Pain builds character. Character builds relationships. Relationships build business.

All this is true.

I heard one guy dressed in cool black clothes with a cool headset microphone say that we should embrace failure. Embrace failure so we can get ahead. I'm pretty sure he was full of poop.

I was once fired from a project. It was a big, high profile project. I learned all sorts of lessons from the event. When I see the politics of a project moving sideways now, I don't embrace the failure. I fear the possibility of that failure repeating. Almost as much as spiders. Fear of failure causes motivation and action!

The number one reason you are reading this book is that you fear your business will fail financially. That is a healthy fear. You should fear business failure. If you do fail, then learn. We all fail. Learn the lessons and move on.

But if you can out-think the circumstances and avoid failure, well, do so. Duh.

The Money Mood Cycle

Most businesses ultimately fail due to lack of money. As a result, low cash levels cause huge stress. This stress is the fear of financial failure.

Stress puts us in a bad mood. We can fake it for a while, but eventually we wear out and show the signs of stress.

When cash is plentiful, the relief from stress puts us in a good mood. We remember that we entrepreneurs are optimists by nature. This business will succeed. I will succeed. Life will be awesome! Rainbows and unicorns!

Then we spend some of that money investing in our business. Angela needs a new computer. Tim needs some new production equipment. I need a new office chair, one of those plush leather racecar chairs with speakers in the head rest and buttons on the armrests.

Before long, we have less cash.

When the cash gets tight again, we are under stress and in a bad mood. We stop having fun.

A bad mood damages our relationships. Staff walk on eggshells. Deadlines are missed. Clients become unenthused with our work. Relationship strain damages our business. We then do less business, which results in even less cash.

Clients delay payment on invoices because they like their other vendors more. We call upset because we desperately need to be paid.

Then one day it seems every client pays their bill all on the same day. And the cycle repeats.

The Money Mood Cycle is a rollercoaster for your checkbook, for company morale, for client satisfaction, and for your business growth.

It's also a rollercoaster for your health. That flat stretch at the end of the rollercoaster is where you are resting in the hospital after a major medical event. If you're lucky, you can take the ride again. If not, you will be ejected from the rollercoaster. I know what I'm talking about. I've had two strokes. I have the t-shirt.

The Money Mood Cycle is no joke. I want you to get it under control. If you are going to damage your health by doing something stupid, then at least let it be too much bacon... if there is such a thing.

Bacon Bits

- Control your revenue in. If you sell a product, always take payment as you sell, not at a later date, unless you know and trust your customer with your life.
- Seasonality will vary your revenue in. Understand your sensitivity to seasonality. Prepare for off seasons.
- We fear failure more than anything. Low cash levels stirs our fear of failure and increase stress.
- Stress causes irritability, damage to relationships, and decrease in business.
- Stress can kill you. Literally.
- Fluctuations in cash flow and stress levels create the Money Mood Cycle.

Chapter 4: Basic Cash Flow
You worked for it, so keep tabs on it.

"To handle yourself, use your head; to handle others, use your heart." -Eleanor Roosevelt

"What you focus on is what you get." - Bob Burg

Years ago, as a young adult, I helped with a local Boy Scout troop. The fire department offered to host us for a demonstration. In the glory of our pre-litigious culture, we were allowed to play with the equipment, chop mock walls with axes, sit inside the trucks and flip the switches, and wear the gear.

They set up a hose for the kids to try. Those hoses are under immense pressure and shoot water a good mile or two, so it seemed. The kids were having difficulty holding onto the hose, so I was called in to man the nozzle.

I'm a big dude. I stand at six feet tall and weigh in at over an eighth of a ton. I was younger then and spent time lifting weights in the gym. Oh yeah, I was just the guy to handle this beast.

I donned my loaner jacket and helmet and approached the professional fireman holding the fire hose. Some young teenagers followed behind me.

"Are you ready for this?" he asked.

"Absolutely," I said with a cocky grin. I could hear other firefighters talking to the teens as they picked up their spot on the hose behind me.

"Hold it tight. If you lose your grip, it can whip you in the face, groin, anywhere you're not protected. It somehow knows."

"Got it," I said, a little more serious now. I lowered my face shield.

"This is the valve handle. It's real simple. Turn this way for more water, turn that way for less. Hard to screw up. Got it?"

"Got it," nodding now with confidence. I could feel the hose jerk once or twice as the teens got their grips.

"Use this hand to hold the base of the nozzle. Grip tight."

I nodded again, ready to go.

"Okay, we're going to pressurize," he said as he let go and backed off. "Three, two, one…"

The nozzle bucked in my hands as the water was turned on somewhere behind me to pressurize the hose. The hose fabric turned rock hard. A few of the teens grunted as they were pushed around. It sounded like one fell, but all I could think about was the valve in my hand. It was still shut, with just a trickle coming out of the nozzle. I was ready to blast some high-pressure water!

"Here I go," I yelled.

Somewhere behind me I heard, "Open it slo…"

Too late. I cranked that valve lever all the way over.

Holy mother of bucking broncos!

The nozzle jumped up and down with a life of its own! I sprayed the ground between my feet and was immediately blinded by mud and chunks of sod. I sprayed the sky and it rained on everyone. I somehow sprayed myself under the face shield and lost both my contacts and any need to drink for days.

How did I keep my footing?

I regained my wits and cranked the nozzle closed. The jet of water slowed back to a trickle. Ripping off my helmet to clear my face, I could hear shouts from the other scout leaders and firefighters.

All the teens were lying on the ground covered in mud.

I heard one firefighter say, "Thank the good Lord we gave him the trainer hose."

Trainer hose?

Cash flow for many small businesses is just like a fire hose: full blast or a trickle. It's hard to handle, so owners want the controls simple to operate.

There are two basic ways most small businesses keep tabs on their cash flow. Periodically, their accountant sends some reports with fancy names. Otherwise, the owner just watches the checkbook.

Hindsight Is Twenty-Twenty

Accountants, God bless them, deliver to you multiple routine reports at some period you have specified. I get mine monthly, but many businesses get them quarterly. Typical reports include:

- Asset Balance Report
- Liability Balance Report
- Profit and Loss Report or Income Statement
- Cash Flow Statement
- General Ledger Report

They may be called something different by your accountant, but they all say pretty much the same thing: how your business is doing financially up to the time the report was generated.

Asset reports will list all the things your company owns or is owed. They may include things like cash, bank account balances, accounts receivable, stockholder loans, equipment, inventory, real estate, and goodwill. If this is all added up at the end, you'll see a pretty nice number. But hold your horses. This isn't necessarily what your business is worth. That calculation is better left in the hands of a professional business broker.

Liability reports will list all the things your company owes, such as credit cards, principle on loans, and stockholder equity. This report total will match your asset report total. The reason they match it this formula: assets minus liabilities equals equity. I'm pretty sure the real reason is that accountants like numbers wrapped up cleanly and tied with a bow. True story.

Income statements list gross income (revenue), cost of goods sold, gross profit, business operating expenses, and net taxable income (net profit). These reports may be for an individual time period but are often listed out in monthly columns for the year. The noted profit and loss at the bottom of these columns is supposed to be the actual profit or loss you made. But it's not. Those numbers are really the taxable profit or lack thereof. As noted in chapter one, these reports are not cash in the bank but rather important puzzle pieces in figuring tax liability.

Cash Flow Statements tell the story of how cash is moving around your business. How much came in due to company sales? How much was spent on operations? How much was used for investing in business growth and how much was borrowed? How much was in your bank accounts? A Cash Flow Statement can reflect the financial health of your company.

General Ledger reports are pretty much the same thing as your checkbook register and bank statement. You'll remember bank statements as those envelopes that build up in a pile next to your coffee pot at home. A general ledger is your side of your bank statement.

The accountant or CFO reading this book just rolled their eyes. I love getting mail but hold off on sending me that letter for now. This book isn't for you. Financial experts already know how to handle money. This book is for new businesspeople who don't. So easy on the hate mail. If you must send something, include cookies.

Read these accountant reports. They're critical to understanding where your business has been and knowing whether or not you should disappear into the back woods of Maine before you get your tax bill. Talk to your accountant routinely. They're super smart and will provide you important guidance.

But remember, all those reports concern what your company did up until the moment the report was generated. Those reports will tell you bupkis about what is happening right now or what is about to happen.

Keeping a Checkbook Register

Many small businesspeople ignore all those financial reports. If you read them, you probably skip to the bottom to see if you have made money. It sure is nice to make money.

But you know those accounting reports aren't the same as cold hard cash. Even if they were, the information is, at best, three weeks old. For most businesspeople, they're several months old.

To know if you're making money, you do it the same way I did before I learned better. I opened the general ledger and looked to see how much money we actually had available to spend. Simple and accurate.

Careful now. Today, your bank account balance is available on your phone with up to date account information anytime, anywhere, except the back woods of Maine. Cell signal isn't great up there. That's why I go.

I said I checked the general ledger, also known from now on as your checkbook register, because that's how real people talk. You or your bookkeeper have been writing checks. Not all of those checks have been deposited and drawn on your account yet. Some people will hold onto checks for a crazy long time. Your checkbook register will be different than your bank statement.

Is your checkbook register a crumpled up ball of receipt and carbon copy checks in a cute little basket on the back of your desk? If you aren't keeping your checkbook register up to date, then you are right now considering the fetal position because you have no idea how much money you really have. Don't retreat to your couch with a half-gallon of ice cream and *Friends* reruns. Well, not yet. Instead, you need to learn to track your checking account expenses in your checkbook register. It's the first step to keeping track of your finances.

The Checkbook Register

I was taught how to keep a checkbook register by my mother back in the eighties. Today, some kids are taught in high school. A checkbook register is simple math, so don't be afraid. Anyone in business can and needs to do this.

Here is how to do it, step by step. If you already know how to keep a checkbook, skip ahead to page 41. Or read this as a refresher. You decide, since you are the one with this book in your hands.

If you have a very small business, keep your checkbook in the checkbook register your bank gives you when you open a checking account. They come in little vinyl booklets with checks on one side and the register on the other. If you are feeling a little more adventurous, use a spreadsheet. Mid-sized businesses sometimes use three ring binders filled with sheets that only have three entries per page with room available to record lots of information about each expense or deposit. There are many software applications as well that will do even more for you, such as QuickBooks. If you have never kept an accurate checkbook register, I recommend you start with the provided paper checkbook register.

When you order checks, skip the checks with carbon copies. Sure, you have a copy of each check as proof you wrote it, but these days, banks keep a digital copy of every check anyway. You can access them anytime. If, for some reason, you have a concern that someone might challenge a particular check, – which has never happened to me – take a picture with your phone. The reason you should skip the carbon copy checks is they provide temptation to not update your checkbook register when you write a check. Human behavior is the chief cause of disorder, so create systems to avoid error. This is what entrepreneurs do.

Record every dollar which comes in to or out of your business in the checkbook register. Your checking account is the financial foyer of your business. Everything that comes in is deposited to your checking account. Everything that is spent is spent from the checking account. Everything in or out goes through the checking foyer.

Record everything. Do it without fail. Do it when it happens. Keep your check register up to date, always.

Record the date, check number, who it was written to, and the amount. If your checkbook register has a space for a memo or note, use it. Months later, you may not remember what it was for. Update the running total.

The running total is your go-to number. It's how much money is at your disposal in your checking account. The checking account balance on your phone app is not the correct number because it doesn't account for the checks you have written but haven't yet been cashed at the bank.

Your checkbook register tells you how much money you have if you still plan to meet all your pending financial obligations. If you're not planning to do that, throw this book away and don't tell anyone you know me.

At home, where my wife and I both have access to the account, we like to keep a buffer. A hidden cash buffer is when you deposit some money into your checking account but you don't record it in the checkbook register. Lisa and I started with a $100 hidden cash buffer. As our household income increased and our children turned into expensive eating machines, we increased our buffer. We now have a $500 buffer. Even if the checkbook register reads $0, we really have another $500 in case we both write checks without talking first. That shouldn't happen, but life does.

At work, I don't recommend a hidden cash buffer. Your checkbook register should read exactly how much money you have in the checking account at your disposal. One person should be in charge of the checkbook register, so a hidden cash buffer shouldn't be necessary. Instead, just make sure the checkbook register has a positive value at all times, which is simply a cash buffer.

How much cash buffer you keep in your checkbook register is up to you and your business model. At Main-Land, payroll is our largest expense because of what we do. We pay our people well, as they very much deserve. They also need to be paid every week. So, we try to keep a pretty healthy buffer. As the months pass, you will come to understand how much of a cash buffer you need for your business.

Remember, always keep your checkbook register up to date. The balance is the working cash at your disposal. You must know that number. Keep it up to date like your bacon depends on it.

Just kidding about skipping ahead. Go back to page 38 and read it for a refresher. I promise it won't hurt you. Probably.

Reconciling

Next, you need to have confidence that your checkbook register is correct. Mistakes do get made.

Learn to balance your checkbook monthly with your bank statement, also known as reconciling your checkbook register. Reconciling is nothing more than comparing your checkbook register to your bank statement, entry by entry, to make sure they are the same. These skills are taught in high schools around the world, or should be, so you can do this.

Start by finding the first expense or deposit for the checking account on the bank statement. It should be dated on the first of the month, or shortly thereafter. Look at how much it was. Then turn to your checkbook register and find the expense by scanning for the same amount. It may be dated the same day or earlier. It may be dated the previous month or the month before if the check recipient was slow to deposit it. Once I find the expense or deposit, I cross it off the bank statement with a red pen *and* mark it with an "R" in the checkbook register. That one matches. Reconciled.

I don't scan for check numbers, recipients, or other data. Only some of the expenses will be checks with a number. The rest will be debit card, ATM, and other expenditures, so the check number is only helpful in confirming. The recipient you wrote in the checkbook register may not read the same on the bank statement, especially if you used a debit card. The date will rarely match due to the time delay between you spending to the recipient depositing. So, scan for amounts, which are often unique for that month.

You know what to do next. Move to the next line on the bank statement and repeat, matching the amount of the next item to the same item in the checkbook register. Red pen and "R." Continue item by item. Do this for all expenses and deposits the bank statement has for your checking account.

What if your bank statement has an item that isn't in your checkbook register? Uh oh. On your first pass, just circle this entry on the bank statement and move on.

What if your checkbook register has something that isn't on the bank statement? This may not be a mistake, but rather a delay on the recipient's part.

When you get to the end of the bank statement, pat yourself on the back. Then go back to the bank statement and look for anything that was missing. Rarely does every item get crossed off on the first pass. You circled them on the bank statement, so they are easy to find now. Often an entry you thought was missing in your checkbook register wasn't missing but was visually lost in the list of numbers. Now it's easily found because it wasn't marked with an "R".

Occasionally, despite what I said about immediately recording expenses, you will still forget to enter an item in your checkbook register. Oops. Consider your hand slapped. Enter it now, mark it with an "R", and cross it off the statement.

Once in a great while, an entry on the bank statement is a bank error or a hacked account. That triggers a call to the bank, which may have proof of the transaction or may clear the entry on their end.

When all the checking account bank statement entries have been crossed off, you have a reconciled checkbook register. Your total at the bottom of your checkbook register is validated. You can rely on it.

Occasionally, an entry never shows up at the bank. If it's a check, maybe the recipient never deposited it. Maybe they lost it. Some people are terribly disorganized. Otherwise, look for a duplicate entry. I sometimes mistakenly enter a transaction in the checkbook register twice, usually because I haven't had enough coffee.

That may sound like a ton of work. It is work, but not a ton. Even today, with an awesome CAO on staff, I spend about an hour reconciling our company checkbook register each month. I do it personally for accountability, because I'm a nerd, and in order to get a gut level feel for my money. An hour a month is worth knowing this all-important resource down to the dollar. For this reason, I don't recommend just comparing the monthly totals. Reconcile line by line to *understand* your money situation.

If you can afford a CFO, then hire one and make them do this task. Until then, I recommend you, the business owner, do this personally.

If you get stuck, call your local bank manager for help. Ask nicely. If they won't help you, get a new bank and call your accountant. Classes are available almost everywhere; check out your local Adult Ed. And online there is this thing my kids love called YouTube. They watch other people play video games, which I am pretty sure is missing the point of video games. I only use YouTube to fix the stuff my kids break, but a quick query shows about a metric ton of help there for reconciling checkbooks.

The rest of this book assumes you have a working checkbook register and you reconcile it monthly. If you are not, stop reading and go do it right now.

But make coffee first.

The Checkbook Method of Financing

The checkbook register is the all-important performance indicator for your business.

If the checkbook register is going up, the business is doing well. If the checkbook register is going down, the business is faltering. Business owners watch their checkbook balance closely because it shows both how much money we really have and because it tells us if we are winning or losing at business.

That is the *checkbook method of financing*. Just watch the checkbook register total. Forget financial planning. Skip the dreaded budget. Lose the profit-loss statement. All that really matters is the checkbook balance.

Most small business owners only use the checkbook method of financing. Why spend time budgeting when this works just fine? I know businesses that have successfully operated for decades on the checkbook method of financing. Why do anything more? You don't have time for anything more. You are too busy. Right?

The checkbook method of financing leads directly to the rollercoaster of the Money Mood Cycle. Remember that from chapter 3? When the checkbook is high, life is good, and you spend money happily. When the checkbook is low, life is bad, and you get grumpy. Grumpy business owners lose customers. Truth.

Also, there is no plan to handle profit. At the end of the year, all your money will be gone, spent on your business. Even if you have a high checkbook balance come December, you spend it on business stuff to avoid taxes, which is the advice of many accountants.

I find Murphy strikes hard in December, so you might spend leftover cash on cleaning up his mess. Or, fun fact, Christmas comes in December every year. You had a great year, so why not splurge on a new truck, you know, for the family?

Lastly, but most dangerously, taxes aren't due on December 31st. Taxes are due on April 15th. If you have nothing saved for taxes at the end of the year, then you have exactly three- and one-half months to save up for taxes on profits you spent twelve months earning last year. This is a business killer.

The checkbook method of finances is easy. You keep your checkbook register up to date anyway. You are doing that, right? So, with one glance at your cash on hand you can make an intuitive estimate on whether things are good or bad.

But easier and faster is not necessarily stronger and better. What if there are financial methods better than the checkbook method of financing? What if you could do just a little bit of math to create financial safety, anti-depressants for your money mood cycle, and profit left over for you? Profit. Like actual money as a reward for all you've done.

Math?

For some people, I just said a dirty word. Rest assured. There is math for people who like math, and there is math for people who ... oooo, look, a butterfly!

Bacon Bits

- Review your accountant's reports to understand your business, but be aware they tell you what *has* happened, not what *is* happening or what will happen.
- Keep your checkbook register up to date at all times. Like, always. Know how much cash you have available.
- Reconcile your checkbook every month. Do this line by line. Do this yourself until you can afford to hire a CFO.
- The Checkbook Method of Finances is using the checkbook to know what is financially happening right now without any way to plan for what will happen later.

Chapter 5: Personalities

There is more than one way to skin a cat. Gross.

"I can't change the direction of the wind, but I can adjust my sails to always reach my destination." -Jimmy Dean

"Life is 10 percent what happens to me and 90 percent of how I react to it." -Charles Swindoll

I coordinate and teach financial principles to families in our church and community once each year using Financial Peace University. FPU is my favorite way to teach these principles to families who are financially struggling or just need a financial refresher. People of many stripes attend: young and old, high and low earners, families with kids and singles that get to sleep at night.

FPU is a commonsense approach to handling home finances. I love this product put out by Dave Ramsey at Ramsey Solutions. I can't help but plug this program. I didn't get paid to do so, and I don't get paid to put on his class. My wife, Lisa, and I took the course ourselves, learned the seven baby steps, and gained real hope for our financial future. I have personally witnessed hundreds of people do the same as I have coordinated this program over the years. Learn more at www.daveramsey.com/fpu today. If you live in Maine, and why wouldn't you, then call Fayette Baptist Church at (207) 685-9492 for the next scheduled class. We hold one every winter.

If a family asks financial questions, I'll help if I can. But I also refer them to FPU. At the end of the nine-week course, I always offer one free counselling session to any attendee who has more questions or wants help with their particular situation. Well, not free. I demand cookies.

I was once counseling a young couple in our church. They brought cookies. They had lots of student loans, consolidated in this poopy debt program that based their monthly payment on their income. Their monthly payment was less than their monthly interest. Their loan principle had increased since graduation!

As this couple sat before me, I could see the fear in their eyes. Some quick spreadsheet wizardry showed they would still have those student loans past retirement, if they ever could retire.

We were knee to knee at a folding table to solve this problem. We dove into the numbers. I love numbers. Unlike people, numbers do what they're told. She clearly loved numbers, too. As we poured over the spreadsheets of their incomes and their expenses, her eyes sparked with interest and excitement. She nodded enthusiastically as I pointed out one figure or another on the papers. We were practically forehead to forehead over the math.

After some time this way, deeply focused on the data, I noticed her husband wasn't taking part in our work. He sat back and low in his chair. His hands were in his pockets. The fear in his eyes was replaced by a distant look. He was even slightly smiling.

"You okay, bub?" I asked.

"Huh? Yeah, sorry. Thinking about something else," he replied in his drawn-out Maine accent.

"What were you thinking about?" I challenged, only playful on the surface. I value my time. I could have been at home eating ice cream and watching *Friends*.

"Gronkowski versus Bruschi. Who would Tom Brady prefer to be tackled by?"

Thinking as quickly as I could, I quipped, "Bruschi. Gronk would kiss him on the cheek after the sack."

We chuckled a little, then immediately launched into football talk. Who was the Patriots' all-time best player? We quickly agreed Brady was MVP, but as we launched into offensive drive versus defensive turnovers, I was caught short by a chill down my spine.

A quick glance at his wife and it was all over. I know that look. I've earned it many times.

"Ty Law was best," she finalized. "Now, what do you think about this number here?"

We finished the session. Not only did they figure out how to knock down their student loan debt in a reasonable timeframe, but as of this writing they have paid off over $30,000! They will be free of that shackle before they hit thirty. Now that's great game play!

Ahem. Bruschi was best.

"There Are Two Kinds of People"

There are not two kinds of people. As of this writing, there are nearly eight billion kinds of people. Dividing the planet into only two kinds is narrow, polarizing, and not a little unkind.

I do it all the time.

I'm not a formal student of psychology. I don't know all the different shades of color that drive people. But I do know I am generally a simple person and you probably are too. I know we can learn something from the exercise of segregation of motivations. So, dividing into two is the simplest of segregations. I learn from the generalization and admit people are too complicated to follow it absolutely.

At that FPU class, we learn there are two kinds of people: nerds and free spirits. In the above partly true story, she was the nerd. He was the free spirit.

Nerds

Nerds have a bad reputation. Nerds are those kids in school who played chess during recess, carried their trombone on the bus, and sat alone at lunch. If they sat in a group, they laughed at poop jokes and argued about star destroyers versus warping starships. If you know what I am talking about, I have bad news for you.

Nerds like math and literature. Nerds know about fractions and grammar. Nerds are smart. Nerds are not cool.

Students, be careful how you treat a nerd. Someday you will work for one.

Nerds like control. Nerds see chaos and tremble. We just cannot help but attempt to make sense of it, to structure the ebb and flow of life.

I'm a nerd. There, I confess. I had a trombone. A day spent deeply focused on a single spreadsheet, complete with multiple worksheets, charts, and graphs is a day well spent. If I need to calculate something, I prefer to program a spreadsheet to do it in lieu of a calculator because I can then use the spreadsheet the next time the math issue comes up. I don't actually save any time, because the next time I'll edit the spreadsheet with equations and color coding. That's super nerdy.

Nerds are important. When something needs to be planned, go to a nerd. Good administrators? Nerds. Like your car fast? Designed by a nerd. Reading this right now? Written by a nerd. Edited by a grammar guru nerd. Even the cover was designed by a really great nerd I hire all the time.

If you're not sure if you're a nerd, ask your spouse. They know. Trust them on this one.

Being a nerd isn't bad. Embrace nerdom. Use your ability for deep focus to succeed. Just don't expect everyone to know that star destoyers are better. Some people are not nerds.

Free Spirits

Free spirits live life. They live it hard, fast, and without regret. They may seem like they are chasing one butterfly after another, but there's more to it.

Chasing butterflies is an art. Which butterfly is best? Can that butterfly over there be caught? Not being sure, a free spirit will dash off to try. In moments, well, look at that, there's a better butterfly over there!

Nerds look at this prancing about in wonder and sometimes disdain. But chasing butterflies is fun! They are beautiful, wonderful creations that, I hate to tell you this, eat poop. But forget the poop, because they fly all zig-zagged and loopy, full of color and life. Free spirits you see, must chase and catch butterflies.

When they catch one, they stare in awe and wonder at the colors and patterns. They've already forgotten about the poop. Butterflies are awesome!

A free spirit will bring you that butterfly with a loving smile.

As I write this, I can hear my wife roll her eyes. Butterflies? Really? She tested nerdier than I, and that's saying something. She is a nerd who hates math. Yes, there is such a thing. She is also an excellent writer, organizer, and a world class grammar guru. If you like this book, leave a review where you bought it, pretty please, and make sure to mention Lisa, because she's why you like it.

Now, before you consider free spirits handicapped in the art of business, consider sales, client relations, marketing, invention, innovation, and team building. Replace the word "butterfly" with "customer." You see where I'm going with this.

If you think you aren't a nerd, then you're a free spirit. You would never confess to being a nerd. Seriously, why would anyone strive to be a nerd? Earlier, you got to the section on the checkbook register and skipped ahead. You loved my joke, but kept moving forward. Skimming technobabble is an art form for free spirits.

Before anyone is offended for being labeled a nerd or a free spirit, take a deep breath. Few people are totally nerdy or totally free spirited, and those that are probably don't own a thriving business. People are bulbous bags of emotional goo. Many people lean nerd. Many people lean free spirited. I tested nerd but am close to the middle.

I mentioned a test. Want to know how you land on the scale? Take FPU. Seriously.

Nerds and Free Spirits with Cash Flow

Nerds tend to be conservative with their money. They plan ahead and know future expenses are coming. Nerds using the checkbook method of financing like to see the balance grow so they can cover those expenses.

Free spirits never met a dollar they didn't want to put to work. Entrepreneurs live this way. Every dollar is a chance to chase a butterfly. They know they have future expenses. They may intend to plan ahead, but sometimes fail to do so adequately.

As a result, nerdy business owners tend to have a different cash flow than free spirited business owners.

Free spirits, brace yourselves. I am about to drop a graph on you.

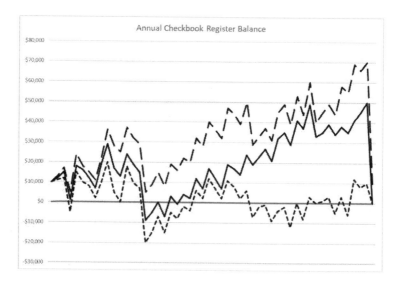

This example chart shows a small business checkbook register balance throughout a year.

Say the business starts the year with $10,000 in the checkbook. Some weeks the business makes money, some weeks the business loses money. Hopefully the balance increases generally over the year, as shown in the solid line above, drafted for a typical average business operating on the checkbook method of finances.

See all those ups and downs? Welcome to the money mood cycle. It actually looks like a rollercoaster.

See the big drop about a third of the way in from the left? That is April 15th. That was Uncle Sam with his hand in your wallet.

See the big drop in December? That is your accountant telling you to buy some stuff for your business so next April won't suck so bad.

And see where it dropped to zero at year end? That's because business owners plan to roll some cash buffer into January, but year-end business purchases and year-end staff bonuses seem to always eat away everything.

If the example business owner is nerdy, they might follow closer to that top long-dashed line. They planned a bit. In December, they consulted with their awesome accountant then thoughtfully purchased a few of those things they planned. And nerds land at the starting balance for the beginning of next year, because they are nerds. And a nerd drew the graph.

Main-Land's graph looked exactly like the nerd graph for years, albeit with a different number scale.

If the example business owner is free spirited, they might follow closer to the lower short dashed line. They have a higher tolerance for risk and a lower motivation to plan ahead. Free spirits aren't worse businesspeople. In fact, free spirits tend to make great businesspeople. They just don't see the point of holding that much money for long.

This chart shows a small business using the checkbook method of financing. Whether nerd or free spirit, average or extreme, they all end up in the same place at the end of year: nothing, or next to nothing.

Something on this chart is missing. It's something important. Where is the reward for your risk, hard work, and stress? Where is the profit?

Whether you're a nerd or a free spirit, the checkbook method of finances does not plan for profit. That's why you've not had consistent profit.

Making Profit

There are better ways to run your business finances.

For nerds, we'll do some math and planning. We will use an age old but often neglected method to track, control, and manage business cash flow. This will be the Bottom-Line Profit method. It is safe, secure, mathematical, and provides full control of your money.

For free spirits, we will use a different method that is simple to use on the fly. This is the Top-Line Profit method.

Don't worry, free spirits. No one can make you do anything. This is a control-free zone. You'll still get to use the checkbook method of financing, just like you always have.

Either way, nerd or free spirit, you'll be able to win with your business finances so you can keep the IRS at bay, buy what you need to grow your business, and take some home for your family.

And maybe a new truck.

Bacon Bits

- Nerds like to math stuff and plan ahead.
- Free spirits like unfettered spending of their money.
- Whether nerd or free spirit, the checkbook method of financing provides no way to ensure profit.
- Because nerds and free spirits like to do things differently, two methods in the following chapters are proposed to control cash flow: Bottom-Line and Top-Line methods.

Chapter 6: The Bottom-Line Profit Method
Planning with a budget.

"A budget is telling your money what to do instead of wondering where it went." -Larry Burkett

"Give me six hours to chop down a tree and I will spend the first four sharpening the axe." -Abraham Lincoln

Just before Lisa and I were married, we attended marriage counseling with Pastor Darryl Whitmer. Darryl was her childhood pastor, and today runs AIIA, a Christian apologetics ministry in Monson, Maine. He was about to marry us in a beautiful white New England church on a hill, so he insisted on some time with us for pre-marital counseling.

Darryl is very wise. During one session, he asked many questions designed to make us think about how marriage was going to work. Many of those discussions revolved around relationship, lines of communication, and commitment. I am ashamed to admit we took very little he said to heart. We would learn the hard way in the coming years.

However, one question was easy to answer.

"Who is going to run the household finances?" he asked.

"Oh, that will be me. I'm good at math," I assured him. Lisa nodded agreement.

I said it with finality. This wasn't up for discussion. I graduated from engineering school at the University of Maine. I could make numbers dance. I knew what I was doing and was good at it.

My attitude, I have found with some life experience, isn't uncommon for a twenty-year-old full of himself. Darryl easily sensed my bravado and gave me his famous eye-sparkling grin. But he was wise enough to move on to the next topic. I wouldn't have listened to any math or financial advice then.

What would a pastor know about math that an engineer would not? Right?

I ran our household finances for years, using a modified checkbook method of finances. I kept a checkbook register and reconciled it most months. But I rarely checked it before a purchase. I bought what I wanted and figured out how to pay for it later. Usually, that involved credit cards.

We bought a car for each of us and had two payments. We rented for a while, then bought a 5,000 square foot house with a sizable mortgage. This was long before the housing crisis of 2008, so mortgage money was easy to obtain. I even took a loan on my 401k for the down payment. This three-story mansion had five bedrooms, five baths, and a live-in apartment. We had one child at the time.

I could afford it. I landed a good job with a sizable company where I performed engineering work on building sites across the state.

As work stress and family stress built up, our attention to finances took a back seat. Three or four months would pass without reconciling the checkbook. We started to live off the running total as stated by the bank, which, at that time, we could easily obtain at the drive-up ATM. It was almost prehistoric.

We fell behind on payments. We bounced some checks. Collectors started calling. How did this happen when I made a good salary?

After a fiery "discussion" with a correctly concerned wife, I ceded the responsibility of our finances to Lisa. Despite my fun at her expense, she can do math just fine. She just doesn't like it.

She would have succeeded. I don't doubt it because she succeeds at everything. She's totally awesome. But now that I wasn't responsible for our finances, I had no reins and no qualms at buying what I deserved. I was the primary bread winner. I deserved to get whatever I wanted. In effect, I undermined her like a defensive end tackling a quarterback at the knees.

We fell so far behind on our payments that we ignored the phone every evening between six and nine. We just wouldn't answer it because we knew a well-trained collector was on the other end.

With another child pending soon, we sold the mansion and moved back into a small apartment. That freed up enough money to at least stay current on the credit card payments.

With a little more maturity gained in those years, and the emotional scars to show for it, we learned frugality. After our second son was born, Lisa was diagnosed with type 1 diabetes, which is the scary kind requiring daily insulin to stay alive. Diabetes required us to be frugal because diabetes supplies are expensive. We paid off a few credit cards and the student loans with some hefty bonuses from my skyrocketing career. Still, we struggled financially. The stress of life required some soothing purchases, eventually including a house with another mortgage. Rationalization is an acquired skill, well-honed by years of bad behavior.

After twenty-five years of marriage, a whopping $1,250,000 passed through our checking account. Yes, that's seven figures. It boggles my mind. For all that money, what did we have to show for it?

We had two cars, both with payments, one of which was upside down. We had a house with a significant mortgage. Lisa was living with an expensive, incurable disease. We added a third son to the mix, and all three were growing like weeds. Seriously, I should've installed a revolving door on the refrigerator. We saved no money for those boys to go to college. We saved no money for emergencies. We saved no money for anything.

We would have had a negative net worth if my employers weren't so generous with their Individual Retirement Account (IRA) matches. Even that balance didn't leave us with a warm and fuzzy feeling for some future retirement, should we ever be able to retire.

After twenty-five years working at great jobs with respectable, though not glittering, salaries, we had basically nothing to show for it.

Then we attended FPU.

There, we learned how to manage our money instead of our money toying with us. We learned to get out of debt and did so. We learned to save for what we wanted and pay cash. We learned how to prepare for those sprouting spawn to attend college. We learned to plan for a brighter future.

Nothing about this was easy. But it worked. Still does, every time.

At the heart of managing our money is the *budget.*

Did you think I would say, "Credit card bonus points?" Did you think I would say, "Started my own business and made gobs of money?" Sorry to be the bearer of bad news. There are no shortcuts to hard work. Even for lottery winners. They have the highest rate of bankruptcy for a demographic group.

Darryl Whitmer and Dave Ramsey, thank you for showing love and wisdom to an unappreciative young fool.

The Budget

When you read the word "budget" did your face pucker a little bit?

Budgets are a noose on your decision making. Budgets will shackle your lifestyle. Budgets are what one person uses to beat another person into financial submission. Budgets are negative. Budgets are all about saying no, no, and no to your hopes and dreams.

None of that is true. None of it. The negative connotation of a budget is just a myth we learned from Hollywood. That place is full of wrong information, except *MythBusters.* Adam Savage, you're the man.

Free spirits, this is to catch your attention as you skim this section. Read this part carefully.

A budget is a plan to achieve your dreams. A budget is a net to catch butterflies. A budget won't constrain you. A budget will set you free.

A budget is just pre-planning your expenditures. That's all it is. It isn't to be feared but should be used as a powerful tool to win at business and your financial life.

There are significant positive outcomes of using a budget.

First, a budget forces you to use your head. Sit down to construct a budget with a full pot of coffee. The first run through a new budget will take some time. Dedicate time to just budgeting. No kids. No staff. No phone calls. No email.

No Facebook. It's time to buckle down, just for a little while. This is important because budgeting uses logic, not emotion. A budget frees you to make decisions with your money without the distractions of emotional stress or outside influence. Better decisions are made with money when you use your head instead of your heart. That happens with a budget.

Second, seeing your financial situation summarized in black and white clarifies. Your cash flow starts to take on a discernable shape. Whether or not you like that shape, seeing is believing. Financial self-delusion is a thing.

Third, a budget decimates the money mood cycle. Cash flow will still fluctuate, and the checkbook register may still get low. However, the fear of running out of money is diminished and then outright destroyed when you have a budget to consult.

Fourth, successfully operating on a budget will give you a raise. The amount of money that flows out of your checking account on restaurants, group gatherings, furnishings, and other stuff will shock the most free-spirited mind into a caffeine-injected budgeting session. A budget highlights your unnecessary spending. A budget shows how people sacrifice their hopes and dreams on fleeting fun and stuff that fades. Budget for yourself and see a 10% to 30% increase to your bottom line. Really.

Lastly, a budget gives hope. We all hope our business will succeed. We all hope we will make money and retire comfortably. We all hope we will win. However, hope without faith is folly. A budget is a rock upon which to build real faith in your financial success. Running a business with real hope lifts you up and energizes you and your business. Everyone will notice.

Have I convinced you? Ease that puckered face. A budget may be work, but it's worth the effort. And, a budget is easy. You learned this math in middle school.

Media

How do you start budgeting once you believe me and take the plunge?

In the simplest form, start with a pad of paper and a pencil. It worked for hundreds of years, and it still works today. If you have a very small business or an aversion to computers, it's best to start this way. You don't need a laptop or expensive software to do a budget. My very first company budget started in this simple way.

I'm a nerd, if you haven't heard, so once I had some thoughts on paper I quickly moved to a spreadsheet. I use Excel spreadsheets because I learned computers on IBM machines. Plus, I'm old enough to remember using DOS. But if Apple or Google is your thing, they both have spreadsheets, too.

Spreadsheets aren't to be feared. Think of it as using graph paper on your computer. Teaching spreadsheets is beyond the scope of this book. Use YouTube, take a class at Adult Ed, or just sit down and start using one. A spreadsheet is simple to learn on the fly.

A budget doesn't require advanced spreadsheet techniques. If you can type text and numbers into the cells, and remember the command =sum(X:Y), which I promise I will explain later, then you know enough to use a spreadsheet to make a budget. This book won't recommend a huge complicated spreadsheet, linked worksheets, long mathematical formulas, or any other egghead stuff. Anyway, if you trend nerd enough, you'll figure all that out on your own.

There is software to build and maintain a budget. Every Dollar from the people behind FPU is a good one. QuickBooks will work as well. There are some expensive software suites for larger businesses, but this book has "Small Business" in the subtitle.

Grab a notebook and a good-ole number two pencil or boot up your laptop and open a spreadsheet. Get ready to budget from the top down.

Start at the Top and Work Your Way Down
The formula for business profit is simple.

Revenue – Expenses = Profit

This isn't like for homes or non-profit organizations. That formula is called the zero-based budget.

Revenue – Expenses = Zero

For business owners, we take on the burden of ownership for profit. So, plan for profit. Revenue – Expenses = Profit!

Revenue

A budget starts at the top with revenue. How much will come in the door next year? Don't include depreciation or other funny accounting money for your small business. That's your accountant's job. Leave them to it. Money that comes in the door is real money. It's money you will deposit in your checking account. It's your financial resource you must manage responsibly.

Most business owners know this number off the top of their head. We like to refer to it as our company size.

"Oh, we're just a little company," someone might say at a business mixer. "We did two million last year." Usually these things are said when talking to someone with a smaller business than them. It's business owner brag and it sucks. I doubt you do it, but I've had it done to me.

Enter your annual revenue amount on the first line of your budget.

This revenue number is gross. Not cat-skin gross, but gross like the total amount that comes in the door before you pay any sub-contractors. Add up all your deposits for the year and you have gross revenue.

The next line is for pass through costs. If you hire sub-contractors, someone else generated that revenue. You must pay them before you spend anything else.

Not all businesses have sub-contractors, but mine does. Main-Land does consulting work on almost all aspects of land. Almost. For example, we have geotechnical engineers who investigate the ground under buildings and figure out how much the ground can support. You may have never considered that, but you don't want to work in a building slowly turning into the Leaning Tower of Pisa. Main-Land doesn't have a drilling rig to core into the ground for sampling. Every time we do a geotechnical investigation, we hire another company to drill holes. We get a bill from the drilling company that we pass through to our client. The drilling company invoice is added to the contracted costs.

Any individual or company that bills you for their work and you pass the bill through to your client is a sub-contractor. This includes any "staff" the IRS says is an independent contractor. Be careful of that stuff. The government bureaucracy has some wiggy rules about independent contractors.

Enter your contracted costs on the second line.

Next, you need to know your net revenue, which is the amount your company makes and can spend on expenses. To get a net revenue, subtract the contracted cost number on the second line from the gross revenue on the first line, and enter it for net revenue on the third line. That is the amount you have to operate your business.

If I lost you, fear not. An example spreadsheet is provided. Read on.

Net revenue is the amount of money your company makes and can spend on expenses. This is your working income, the amount of money you have to operate and stay alive.

Not a nerd? No problem. Try this. Click on the net revenue cell, type the = sign, then click the cell with your revenue number, type the - sign, then click the cell with your contracted number, and hit enter. You just typed in a formula, which will do the math for you.

If your net revenue number is in cell B4 (like the example spreadsheet on the next page), then cell B4 will contain this text: =B2-B3

Magic. Later, if you update your gross revenue or contract costs in cells B2 or B3, the math for net revenue will automatically update for you. I said I was not going to teach you how to operate a spreadsheet, but I couldn't resist showing you. Nerds. Gotta love `em.

Let's consider an example. Say Bob owns a bacon business called Bob's Bacon Bistro. Everyone loves bacon, except maybe the hogs. Bob's business is small but growing.

Bob knows he brings in about $260,000 annually.

Bob has many customers, but one special customer requires delivery by refrigerated hovercraft. Bob wishes he had a hovercraft but makes do with a big pickup. So, he hires Harry's Hovercraft service to do the delivery. This service cost of $24,000 annually is passed through to the customer at their request.

Bob doesn't have $264,000 to operate Bob's Bacon Bistro for the year. He has $240,000.

Bob's Bacon Bistro budget will start like this.

Bob's Bacon Bistro Budget	Annual Budget
Gross Revenue	$264,000
Contracted Costs	$24,000
Net Revenue	$240,000

With a grip on how much money is available to operate a business, it's time to plan how to spend it.

Cost of Goods Sold

At this point, someone will want to talk about cost of goods sold or cost of sales. This is more for accounting than operating your business, but you might see the term on the financial statements provided by your accountant.

Cost of goods sold is the cost to produce your goods or services, including inventory, raw materials, and direct labor in making the goods or providing the service.

The cost of goods sold is often entered below the contracted costs line. Net revenue doesn't include cost of goods sold, so subtract cost of goods sold from gross revenue to lower your net revenue further.

You may want to segregate your expenses into two sections: cost of goods sold and discretionary expenses. Operationally, I do not. Main-Land's cost of goods sold is mostly our salaries, since we provide a professional consulting service. Our staff salaries are shown on a line, easy to find and see. If you choose to segregate this expense, do so with advice from your accountant, since there are tax implications to how this is counted.

If, like me, you choose not to segregate out the cost of goods sold, then just let your accountant do it for you later. Remember, this book isn't Generally Accepted Accounting Principles (GAAP). What I'm teaching are practical methods for you to gain control of your money.

Expenses

Expenses are what you spend to run your company. Every check, every swipe of a debit card, and every time you fork over cash is an expense.

Lumping all your expenses into one or two lines is too little information. That's not budgeting. As the business owner, you need a better handle on your expenses. So, segregate those expenses into categories.

The categories you use will depend on your business. I don't know your business or how you operate it, so create your own categories. But I do know my business, so I can recommend some for you to consider.

Inventory

Whatever you make and sell, you probably don't do so from scratch. Main-Land is a consulting company. We sell our knowledge about how to help people with their land, with engineers, surveyors, and environmental scientists. But even we have some physical inventory we purchase and resell to our clients. Our surveyors need iron pins for property corners. Our scientists need little colored flags to hang in the field to delineate natural resources.

Bob's Bacon Bistro needs to buy pork bellies. Lots and lots of delicious pork bellies. Pork bellies form much of the inventory.

A store buys inventory to sell. A coffee company buys coffee beans. A furniture maker buys wood, leather, and brass tacks.

Whatever you sell, you probably should have an inventory category.

OpEx

Your company will have some obvious operating expenses. The OpEx category will handle these expenses.

Typical OpEx items will include payroll, rent, utilities, and fuel. Also, consider using this for quarterly payroll taxes, insurances, company gatherings, trade organization dues, consulting services (there you go, accountants!), and office supplies.

Office supplies can quickly get out of hand. Main-Land has a great CAO who keeps this under control. Still, we found office supplies became a dumping ground for expenses which didn't belong anywhere else. We ended up segregating those expenses further in order to track and control office supply expenses.

Capital Expenses

Your company has equipment. Whether that equipment is a survey total station (they aren't cameras, stop asking), commercial coffee bean grinders, or high-grade bacon smokers, this equipment will need to be replaced when it breaks down or your company outgrows it.

Capital expenses are often large and can catch a small business unaware. We will address capital expenses later, but for now they deserve a category to themselves.

Lastly, capital for budgeting is not the same thing as what your accountant thinks of as capital. For this book, capital is used more generally as the expensive stuff you need to run your business.

Capital Maintenance

Your stuff will break down. That is what stuff does.

Some stuff can be repaired by an enterprising entrepreneur. Many companies also have that one person that can fix most anything. If you can fix it yourself, cool.

Main-Land has a guy. His name is Ed (name changed because he's a big dude and could hurt me), and it seems he can fix most anything. He can fix our vehicles, our survey equipment, and repair our building. And sometimes he does so, often on the fly and without being asked. But when Ed is fixing something, he's not surveying. So, Ed and I have talked and have an understanding on when it makes sense and when we should just hire someone to do it for us. He has a good head on his shoulders, often making that decision himself.

Until you have an Ed, be careful to spend your time wisely. As the business owner, your time is more valuable than a mechanic's. Unless you own a diesel pickup truck. I love the purr of a diesel engine, but they aren't cheap to maintain.

Marketing

If you want to sell, you must market your product or service. Your future customers need to know about you. Word of mouth is powerful and necessary, but not controllable.

Marketing expenses include advertising in newspapers, trade journals, television and radio, billboards, and other venues.

Giveaways go here, too. Those are the pens, koozies, and other products given away at seminars and trade shows. I once got a calculator and thought I was in heaven.

Golf tournaments are a time-tested way for non-profits to raise money for important causes. Team registration, tee sponsorships, and mulligans are effectively marketing costs.

Main-Land offers a scholarship annually for a graduating high school student going into any technical or building trade field. We feel it's a good way to support our rural area and show our local young people that our field is worthy to pursue. Getting people to relocate to Livermore Falls, Maine is hard to do, so a scholarship is also a way to grow our own future team members. Regardless of our reason, a scholarship is marketing. We put it here.

When marketing through local charitable events, be discerning. The line for non-profit causes never ends. The many opportunities may lead to unprofitability.

A business must spend money on marketing to survive and thrive, so why not spend it where it will also help people in need?

Financials

It takes money to make money, so they say. I'm not convinced. It takes hard work to make money.

Not only is it possible to start a business from scratch on a card table in your living room, but I know businesses that have done so.

Dave Ramsey of Ramsey Solutions claims to have started his business, now with over 900 employees as of this writing, exactly that way. He took no loans. He had no credit cards. He had no money.

He also had no debt.

Starting a business from zero is a very risky thing to do. That's not to say you shouldn't, but rather it isn't for everyone. I marvel at and am inspired by startup entrepreneurs. I don't mind risk, but that's too much for me.

I was neither that enterprising nor educated at the time. I bought my business. Therefore, I have some debt and payments to make.

If you have any loans, put them here in the financials category. This category should also include credit line interest, credit card interest, and bank fees. Some tax savings will go here, too. More on taxes later.

Contingency

A budget is a plan for financial success. A budget isn't a hedge against the unexpected. Things can and will go wrong. Plan for those problems with a contingency category.

Fair warning. The contingency category can become a catch-all category for things you should have anticipated. If it turns out the budget didn't include paying the water bill, that isn't a contingency item, that's an OpEx item and should be entered there. Later, I will show you how to adjust your budget to fix these omissions.

The Budget

An aircraft is controlled by the steering yoke. But that isn't all. An airplane cockpit has a confusing array of buttons, switches, levers and displays. These are the plane's controls. They're called controls because it's what they do to the aircraft.

In the same way, these expense categories of inventory, operating expenses, capital expenses, capital maintenance, marketing, financials, and contingency provide control for the cash flowing through your business.

As an example, Bob's Bacon Bistro budget might look something like this.

Bob's Bacon Bistro Budget	Annual
Gross Revenue	$264,000
Contracted Costs	$24,000
Net Revenue	$240,000
Expenses	
Inventory	$42,000
OpEx	$96,000
Capital Expenses	$20,000
Capital Maintenance	$2,000
Marketing	$8,000
Financials	$36,000
Contingency	$12,000
Expenses Total:	$216,000

Did you notice the net revenue is higher than the expense total? Maybe you said, "cha-ching" in your head? Bob took great risk and put in many hours building Bob's Bacon Bistro. He not only deserves to keep the leftover $24,000, he should. He has earned the profit. More on profit in chapter 11.

Spreadsheet Help.
Under the Total rows, make the spreadsheet do the summing for you. Where it says $216,000 in the example, type in the formula: =Sum(B6:B12) Use your cell addresses, or just click on the cells.
The result should equal the sum. Check it to trust it.

First Timers

If this is your first-time budgeting, don't panic. List the categories out. Decide if you need all of them. Maybe you need more. Not sure? Just guess and get started.

Then think each category through one at a time. Gather your receipts and separate them into categories. Add up each pile of receipts and take a stab at what the category budget should be. Your budget is yours! You can change it later.

For some businesses, the idea of gathering receipts and going through them is daunting. It was for me. Another option is to spend a month just tracking your expenditures. Segregate each expense into the best fit category as they are spent. At the end of the month, take those category totals and multiply by twelve for annual budget numbers.

Budgeting is a time for thinking ahead. Stop and think about expenses coming up. If you know something big always comes up in June but this is February, estimate how much it will be and add it in.

Nerds, you want more data.

First, you want to know everything up front before doing the work. For first time budgeters, forget that. You will not have all the data. You will have to guestimate.

Second, you want more segregation of the data. OpEx will be too broad for nerds. You will want to separate out payroll, rent, utilities, and the like. I went this route and it drove my CAO a little crazy. It's not only acceptable to create line items inside a category, but it's recommended. My OpEx category has 21 sub-categories. Doing this will help define and create the category and will help later when looking to reduce expenses.

Remember a budget is a working document. It won't be perfect on the first try. Expenses will be forgotten. Bad stuff will happen that necessitates going back to update the budget. Just don't create it and forget it. You'll need your budget to ensure profit and to buy big things you'll need to grow your business.

CERA

Embden had a little Boy Scout troop with about six kids, way back when the Atari 2600 was all the rage. I was one of those kids. I started as a Cub Scout and worked my way up to the final rank of Eagle Scout, which I hold to this day. Shout out to the Boy Scouts of my youth.

One year, when I was perhaps eleven, our troop took part in the regional Jamboree with dozens of other small Maine troops. We camped out in a field, learned how to tie various knots, orienteering, and how to build a fire with a bow and sticks.

One morning, while the two volunteer men were cooking breakfast, my friend Daren and I were hanging around. Because we were eleven, we were drawn to the fire as only young boys are. We poked at it, collected stuff around the campsite to see if it would burn or melt, and generally made a total nuisance of ourselves. After being told, "Leave the fire alone," perhaps a dozen times, the scoutmaster had finally had enough.

"Boys!" he bellowed.

The bark in his voice got our attention immediately. We responded with twin, "Yes, sirs."

"You get no bacon this morning."

Despondent, we hung our heads.

He continued, a little more calmly, "Sorry, boys. There's just not enough bacon. Too many hungry boys around who don't play with the fire."

The other man, who happened to be my father, caught on quick. "That's right. But, George, what if we could get ahold of a bacon stretcher?"

"Well, now. That could work. Boys, go over to troop 223 and see if we can use their bacon stretcher."

Alight with renewed hope, we scrambled away to find troop 223. In the tent city, this was no easy task. But eventually we found troop 227, which was close enough.

"Excuse me, sir. Our scoutmaster asked us to see if we could borrow your bacon stretcher."

The man smiled briefly, then rubbed his chin thoughtfully. "I have a double-A bacon stretcher. But the batteries are toast. Go back and see if that'll work."

Upon return and reporting our news, George shook his head and said, "Sorry, that won't do. We need a nine-volt stretcher. Go check with troop 308."

We sensed something wasn't right. We were eleven, not five. But having nothing better to do, we set out to find Troop 308. It turned out they only had a bacon stretcher that ran on generator power.

Troop 45-70 didn't exist, but 457 did. Their bacon stretcher required solar power. It was overcast that morning.

On our last walk back to our own troop, 496, we found the group serving up plenty of bacon and eggs for everyone. We were so happy to have breakfast we didn't care we were the brunt of the morning's joke.

George was a good man. He took good care of us boys and he made great bacon.

If you look carefully at the above budget, you will notice the capital expense category is $20,000. Some capital expenses are relatively small. Some will hit you like a charging boar.

Bob at Bob's Bacon Bistro plans to buy a bacon stretcher this year. Bob knows there's no such thing, but since he's fictional, he doesn't mind. Bob researches bacon stretchers online and inadvertently enters his email on one bacon industrial supply site. Soon he's contacted and later visited by a rotund man who shows him the latest bacon stretching machine. It'll do all the bacon stretching Bob will ever need. It costs $16,000.

Bob's Bacon Bistro brings in about $20,000 a month. Sixteen thousand out of $20,000 would be financially catastrophic.

Bob is smart. He doesn't take out a loan or put the bacon stretcher on a credit card. Instead, Bob starts saving for his bacon stretcher. He wants to make the purchase in ten months. Doing some quick math, he figures out he will need to save $1,600 a month.

Bob could leave the money in his checking account. But money left in a checking account tends to be check fodder. So, Bob goes to his local community bank and opens a new account, which he uses to hold in reserve money for this capital expense. He names it his Capital Expense Reserve Account. The only mouthful Bob wants is bacon, so he shortens it to CERA.

A CERA is just a savings account to park money, which a business is reserving for capital purchases.

Main-Land has a CERA account. We use it for vehicles, expensive technical software, computers, and survey equipment. One account does nicely for all these larger capital expenditures.

A CERA account is behavior control. If a business owner sees the checkbook register growing large, the entrepreneurial part of him starts to itch. Ideas start to form and different ways to grow the business start to tempt. If the money is in a CERA account, the temptation to spend on some lesser venture is mitigated. The business owner spent time crafting the budget and thought this through. If the owner spends the money on something different, no money will be available for the needed capital improvement.

Every month, Bob will transfer $1,600 into CERA. Ten months later, the money is ready for the bacon stretcher.

Bob breaks his annual budget into a monthly budget. Bob's Bacon Bistro budget now looks like this.

Bob's Bacon Bistro Budget	Annual	January Budget
Gross Revenue	$264,000	$22,000
Contracted Costs	$24,000	$2,000
Net Revenue	$240,000	$20,000
Expenses		
Inventory	$42,000	$3,500
OpEx	$96,000	$8,000
Capital Expenses	$20,000	$66
Capital Maintenance	$2,000	$167
Marketing	$8,000	$667
Financials	$36,000	$3,000
Contingency	$12,000	$1,000
Expenses Total:	$216,000	$16,400
CERA		$1,600
Profit	$24,000	$2,000

The capital expense budget for the year was $20,000, but the CERA budget for the bacon stretcher is only $16,000. The remainder goes to whatever other capital improvements might be needed as the year progresses.

Profit

Did you see the profit line? Profit! The small business budget has a plan to ensure profit.

Earlier, the formula for profit was given as Revenue – Expenses = Profit.

Now, the formula is revised to:

Revenue – Expenses – CERA = Profit.

Bacon Bits

- Anticipate revenue for your business. Subtract out contracted expenses, which aren't really yours. What remains is your net revenue.
- Categorize your expenses as makes the most sense for your business.
- Each category may be made up of many individual line items.
- Save for larger business purchases with a Capital Expense Reserve Account (CERA).
- Net Revenue – Expenses – CERA = Profit

Chapter 7: Operating the Budget
Control your money.

"Never quit. It doesn't sound particularly profound, but life constantly puts you in situations where quitting seems so much easier than continuing on." - Admiral William H. McRaven

My middle son, Nathan, loves airplanes and always has. Today he is in college to be a commercial pilot.

When he was seven years old, he saved his money and bought his first remote controlled airplane. He carefully and lovingly assembled it, testing all the servo motors, radio connections, and minute adjustments, which make an RC airplane fly true. He read all about RC airplanes and even joined an RC airplane club. He spent hours watching YouTube videos about RC airplanes.

The day finally came for him to try out the plane. The wind was right, the temperature was right, and the lawn was freshly mowed into an airstrip of sorts. He checked the plane's flaps, ailerons, rudder, and throttle control. It was ready to go. With the family gathered around, he edged up the throttle until the serving-platter sized plane started to move. It was a little herky-jerky at first but then started to roll forward evenly, picked up speed, and finally took off into the air. His little body quivered in excitement, but his eyes were focused with extreme concentration. He banked the plane left, then right, then right some more.

Right into the top of an old apple tree.

I came to the rescue with a tall ladder and a short stick. Shortly thereafter, his mom came to the rescue with ice for my sprained ankle. The plane was dislodged but hit every other branch on the way down. Styrofoam wings broke off and fluttered to the ground. The dog caught the tail assembly and ran off with it.

Nathan, true to his young age and character, cried for a moment, but then immediately set to analyzing what went wrong and how it would fly better next time. He fixed the Styrofoam with packing tape and adjusted the tooth-pocked tail assembly. His mom warned him I would be climbing no more trees. Before long, the plane was in the air again.

Budgeting is like that. You may spend hours or days preparing the perfect budget only to have it crash and burn shortly after you start. In fact, let me assure you, your first budget *will* crash and burn. There will be budget-parts strewn across the proverbial back yard.

After the first month, analyze it. What did you fail to anticipate? What was tracked wrong? Who did you not pay on time?

Then, sit down and do it again.

The next budget will be bad. But not as bad as the first. It will take less time, too. Repeat the analysis and do it again.

And again.

Six months in, budgeting will take little of your time and will yield measurable profit. One of those early Buying Bacon workshop attendees came to me later and said, "Bob, this stuff is not easy, but it's worth it. I have been an entrepreneur my entire life. My family are entrepreneurs. Last month, for the first time in my life, we tracked and kept some real profit."

Nathan is an expert with an RC plane today. Any given Saturday morning, you can find him in a kayak on a small local pond with a table sized pontoon plane etching graceful loops and barrel rolls over the water with the sunrise gleaming orange on the wings. This pretty picture is life with a well-run budget.

Tracking the Budget

At Main-Land, I spend most of a day in December writing next year's budget. I close my office door, set my phone to silent, close my email, and focus deeply. Twenty employees and nearly 100 hungry stomachs depend on me to get this right. Because I'm a nerd, I do a big, detailed budget with categories and sub-categories. We have multiple departments, so each line gets further broken down into department budgets. Most small businesses don't need to go to this extreme and will do fine with half a dozen categories, with sub-categories as desired, which cover the whole company.

Once your budget is built as described in the previous chapter, track your expenditures for the month. As each expense is spent, which category should you allocate it? Use your best judgement.

This isn't done in the checkbook register. This is in addition to the checkbook register. Sorry.

Spreadsheets can make this additional task easy.

In the tracking cell for each category, enter the = sign and the amount. The next amount is added by adding a + after the previous amount and then enter the next expense amount. The cell text will look something like this: =$12.34 + $532.65 + 39.95

The cell will update and give the total: $584.94.

Later additions will further update the total for that cell.

Let the computer do the math.

Every time an expense is entered into the checkbook register, the budget spreadsheet is opened as well. For each expense, the amount spent is entered into the checkbook register to update the balance *and also* the amount is added to the appropriate budget category in the spreadsheet. Failure to update the budget sheet is backsliding to the checkbook method of finances. You know where that got you. This additional work is the only way to win at budgeting.

Main-Land operates this way. First, we enter the expense in the checkbook. Then we enter it into the budget spreadsheet. Really, it only takes a few seconds extra for each entry. Most small business have maybe 200 expenses a month, which is perhaps 1,000 seconds, or less than twenty minutes. Can you spare twenty minutes a month to ensure profit?

Credit cards add a level of complexity. They're convenient to use, but I don't recommend them. First, they're debt. The credit card bill is the last thing to get paid during tough months, exactly when you don't need debt weighing you down. Businesses can be operated with a debit card through your local community bank just as easily, which is what I recommend.

For this discussion, if you have a company credit card, it will get used for all sorts of expenses and span multiple categories. When the card bill comes in, enter the payment into the checkbook register but not the budget sheet. Now, go down through the statement and assign each individual card expense to a budget category line. If there are any fees or interest paid, then they should be entered in the Financial category.

Track expenses for a month and see how you did.

Bob's Bacon Bistro did this for a month. The updated budget spreadsheet looks like this.

Bob's Bacon Bistro Budget	Annual	January Budget	January Real
Gross Revenue	$264,000	$22,000	$18,832
Contracted Costs	$24,000	$2,000	$2,000
Net Revenue	$240,000	$20,000	$16,832
Expenses			
Inventory	$42,000	$3,500	$3,410
OpEx	$96,000	$8,000	$8,650
Capital Expenses	$20,000	$66	$80
Capital Maintenance	$2,000	$167	$180
Marketing	$8,000	$667	$1,325
Financials	$36,000	$3,000	$3,000
Contingency	$12,000	$1,000	$632
Expenses Total:	$216,000	$16,400	$17,277
CERA		$1,600	$0
Profit	$24,000	$2,000	($445)

Uh oh. Bob lost money last month and was unable to make the CERA transfer.

At month end, a business owner should review how it went. What went well? What did not? This analysis leads to all the important questions needed to make business decisions. What happened to revenue? Should marketing be curtailed? Why is OpEx so high?

Revenue Problems

Some businesses have no problem with revenue fluctuations.

Many other businesses work on an invoicing system. The business does the work, the product or service is provided, then an invoice is generated and sent to the customer.

This will shock some readers, but some customers don't pay promptly, or at all.

A scarier revenue problem is a drop in sales. If accounts receivable isn't a problem, check sales.

Most small business owners live so deeply in their business that a revenue problem isn't a mystery. They know the problem and just need to go fix it.

Expense Problems and Recomp

Expenses can be a mystery, especially if a business owner has a bookkeeper and is therefore not writing checks themselves. Categories over budget are alarms for the owner to investigate. What was spent? Did we need it? Could it have been delayed? Can we innovate a different solution?

Whatever the reason, and whether we learn from them or not, some months are in the red. This is why I recommend a healthy amount kept in the checkbook register as a buffer, also known as the operating cash reserve or the target cash balance.

When budgeting month to month, negative months will eat away at the checkbook register buffer. Eventually, the checkbook will become dangerously low. As soon as you have a good month again, the negative number needs to be recompensated to the account.

In the budget, add a "recomp" line. The following month, your profit will be less this recomp amount.

Bob's Bacon Bistro budget now looks like this.

Bob's Bacon Bistro Budget	Annual	January Budget	January Real	February Budget
Gross Revenue	$264,000	$22,000	$18,832	$24,000
Contracted Costs	$24,000	$2,000	$2,000	$2,000
Net Revenue	$240,000	$20,000	$16,832	$22,000
Expenses				
Inventory	$42,000	$3,500	$3,410	$3,500
OpEx	$96,000	$8,000	$8,650	$8,600
Capital Expenses	$20,000	$66	$80	$50
Capital Maintenance	$2,000	$167	$180	$160
Marketing	$8,000	$667	$1,325	$0
Financials	$36,000	$3,000	$3,000	$3,000
Contingency	$12,000	$1,000	$632	$1,000
Expenses Total:	$216,000	$16,400	$17,277	$16,310
Recomp				$445
CERA		$1,600	$0	$3,200
Profit	$24,000	$2,000	($445)	$2,045

Note the recomp line added to the budget. February's budget has the lost $445 added as a line item in order to keep the checkbook balance at a healthy level.

The bacon stretcher is still an important piece of equipment needed to grow the business. CERA is increased in February to catch up.

Bob also changed February's revenue budget. He analyzed why revenue was down in January and realized a customer hadn't paid for a large order. After a polite but firm discussion with the customer, the payment will arrive in February.

Lastly, Bob went through his OpEx budget and realized he forgot his bacon brine secret ingredient. Bob increased his annual and February budget for OpEx, but he didn't want to lose profits. Something else had to give. Since sales are good and he spent money on a new advertisement in January, he felt he could lower his marketing budget for now.

Under the checkbook method of financing, this adjustment would have been made by intuition, if it was made at all. Just as likely, profit would have taken a hit, which would have gone unnoticed.

As February goes along, Bob will track those expenditures as well. His updated budget in February looks like this.

Bob's Bacon Bistro Budget	Annual	Jan Budget	Jan Real	Feb Budget	Feb Real
Gross Rev.	$264,000	$22,000	$18,832	$24,000	$24,981
Contracted $	$24,000	$2,000	$2,000	$2,000	$2,000
Net Revenue	$240,000	$20,000	$16,832	$22,000	$22,981
Expenses					
Inventory	$42,000	$3,500	$3,410	$3,500	$3,523
OpEx	$96,000	$8,000	$8,650	$8,600	$8,513
Cap. Exp.	$20,000	$66	$80	$50	$134
Cap. Maint.	$2,000	$167	$180	$160	$180
Marketing	$8,000	$667	$1,325	$0	$150
Financials	$36,000	$3,000	$3,000	$3,000	$3,000
Contingency	$12,000	$1,000	$632	$1,000	$462
Exp. Total:	$216,000	$16,400	$17,277	$16,310	$15,962
Recomp				$445	$445
CERA		$1,600	$0	$3,200	$3,200
Profit	$24,000	$2,000	($445)	$2,045	$3,374

Indeed, the accounts receivable were paid. Marketing was temporarily curtailed, though he couldn't resist a local Boy Scout golf tournament tee sponsorship. A CERA transfer of $3,200 was made and entered as an expense in both the checkbook register and the budget spreadsheet. And $445 was held for recomping the bad month.

The recomp isn't an expense in the checkbook ledger. But it was entered as an expense in the budget spreadsheet to correctly calculate profit.

The profit formula was provided as:

Revenue – Expenses – CERA = Profit
But with recomp, the formula needs one last update:

Revenue – Expenses – CERA – *Recomp* = Profit

Bob's Bacon Bistro made a profit in February. That's almost as sweet as bacon drizzled in maple syrup. No? Try it sometime.

Repeating the Budget

Remember the story in the beginning of this chapter? My son Nathan didn't give up. When things went sour, he learned and kept going.

Do the same with your budget. The first month will be a disaster. The second will be bad. The third will have some challenges. By the time the fourth month comes along, it's just a little work. At six months, you'll wonder what the big deal was.

Will This Work?

Yes, I know budgeting works. This is how I operate finances at my own company. I have for years.

Further, my home budget looks very similar and is operated essentially the same way.

Budgeting works.

Profit

The budget will show the profit for the month as a wonderful number at the bottom of the sheet. It's the reward for your month's effort. Look at it, smile at it, and know you got it done this month.

Now, what happens with profit money? This isn't some cerebral exercise. The point is to earn and keep some cold hard cash.

In the checkbook method of financing, the profit just sits in the checkbook, bringing the balance up. We already know what an entrepreneur's mind will do with such money. So, there is one final step to budgeting for profit.

Move it.

Chapter 11 deals with where to move it. So, read on. If you decide not to follow those recommendations, that's your prerogative. But at least move profit somewhere else. Open a separate account at your local community bank and get it out of your business checking account. Profit left in a checking account will grow legs and walk.

Bacon Bits

- Track all expenditures in the checkbook register *AND* in your budget sheet. Keep both up to date.
- In the budget, segregate expenses by categories and line items.
- At month end, transfer to CERA.
- At month end, budget for the next month.
- If money was lost this month, add the lost amount to next month's budget as Recomp.
- Revenue – Expenses – CERA – Recomp = Profit

Chapter 8: Budgeting Tips

Improve your budget skills.

"There are two kinds of people in the world. People whose circumstances overcome them, and people who overcome their circumstances." -Dr. Henry Cloud

"I have been impressed with the urgency of doing. Knowing is not enough; we must apply. Being willing is not enough; we must do." -Leonardo da Vinci

Archery is an activity I've enjoyed my entire life.

It started when I was just a little tyke. I honestly don't remember the first time I shot a bow and arrow. I was too young.

Later, archery was reinforced by Robin Hood, the books and cartoon movie, not the garbage of every other Hood movie made since Flynn. Robin Hood stole from a corrupt government and gave back to the taxpayers. Ahem, I digress.

Rambo helped my love for archery, as well. I remain ever grateful to God for all my fingers after my many attempts to strap explosives onto arrowheads. Don't try this but do watch for you boys trying this.

I learned archery safety after nearly killing my grandfather. When I was a middle-schooler, who as a group aren't known for self-restraint, awareness, or thought of any kind, I had launched an arrow straight up, hoping to see how high it would go. Of course, I lost sight of it. Noting the wind direction, I realized it was likely to come down in the back yard of my parent's house. When I ran back there, I was mortified to see my grandfather blithely walking across the large garden back there. I didn't know whether I should call out or not. Would it be better for him to stop and look up? Well, no, that seemed bad. Before I could decide, the arrow thunked down into the soil right next to his back heel. It missed by an inch, max. He continued on his way, oblivious to his near death.

I never told anyone, except you. I'll probably get a call soon from my Dad.

Not wanting to hurt human beings, I took up archery hunting for wild game. My success in this endeavor has been poor in table meat but rich in fun. My latest archery hunting has been for partridge, which are small woodland chickens found in Maine forests. I'll let you know when I actually get one.

There are many methods of shooting a bow and arrow. It nominally starts with sighting through the string to the arrowhead to the target. Today there are compound bows, mechanical sights, lasers, fiber optic pins, spring-loaded arrow rests, string releases, and stabilizers. I know a guy who often hits his own arrows at half a football field range.

I shoot by a method called instinctive archery. I've learned to use a simple bow, pull the arrow back to a specific point on my cheek called the anchor point, sight generally down the arrow, focus on the target, and then release. I don't aim much, but rather release when my gut tells me the time is right. Instinctive archery takes a metric ton of practice. Today, I can hit a paper plate at thirty yards. It won't get me on a team, but it's not bad for an old dubber stalking the woods for thunder-chickens.

I don't remember my father first teaching me this method. I was too young to remember the details, though I do remember specific instructions concerning shooting straight up.

I fondly remember teaching my boys.

I showed them how to stand. I showed them which hand holds the bow and which pulls the string. I showed them how to nock the arrow and hold it in place while drawing it back. I showed them how to find an anchor point. Then I let them shoot.

Invariably, the first arrow would fly wild. The second as well. On the third, as they pulled the string back, I carefully reached over and adjusted their aim. That arrow flew true.

As you struggle with your first budgets, please allow me to adjust your aim, just a little.

Timing

Paying attention to finances is part of a small business owner's job. This isn't something to be shirked. Failure to handle these matters properly will result in eventual failure and closure. I didn't make that up.

How much time should an owner spend on financial matters? It's up to the owner, but here are a few thoughts.

If the business is large enough to have a bookkeeper, a weekly review of the checkbook register will typically suffice. Then a review of the budget sheet twice a month will give the owner direction on revenue and spending trends. This is what I do at my shop. I also present the numbers to our leadership team twice a month so they can make decisions as work progresses. The weekly review takes 15 minutes or less. The twice monthly review takes maybe an additional 15 minutes. This totals an hour and half of my time per month to have a handle on the current company finances and as forecast in the budget. Doesn't this seem a small price to pay to ensure profit?

Most companies bill weekly or monthly. We bill twice a month, though we split them so each client gets a bill once a month. My review of the budget routinely occurs the week after a billing, so my understanding of the numbers is uniform across cyclical cash flow. I find it better to compare apples to apples.

If the business owner is the bookkeeper, then consider the 10/25 principle written about by author and entrepreneur Mike Michalowicz. Many busy owners will pay bills, make deposits, and issue invoices whenever they have the time. They fit in one part on a Tuesday morning and another late on Thursday, half an hour at a time. This is not only inefficient but also stressful. Instead, try making the 10th and 25th of each month, or the nearest weekday, a money day. Schedule it on your calendar. Collect up all the incoming checks and deposit them. Grab the stash of bills and pay them. Review the checkbook register and budget sheet. Fix what needs to be fixed. Then move on with the work of your business knowing everything will be financially safe until the next money day.

Lastly, there is reconciling. It's not fun but it is very necessary. Reviewing the budget and making profit transfers shouldn't happen until after reconciling the checkbook register to both the bank statement and the budget sheet. Reconciling cannot happen until after the month ends, when you get your bank statement. This doesn't mean all the work needs to happen on the first day of the month. Give yourself some time. If using the 10/25 principle, do this on the 10th. At my shop, the CAO has three weeks after the month ends to do the math, report to me, and for me to reconcile. We meet on the third Monday every month to discuss the previous month's finances and verify CERA and profit transfers.

Cash Payments

Most businesses take payment as checks or credit / debit card payments. Sometimes a client will come in to pay an invoice with real cash.

When real cash crosses their desk, the owner's eyes get a little brighter. This isn't because they are thinking about how to hide it from the IRS. Or, not only.

Real cash is a reminder of the coming reward for a profitable business. Cash is tangible, real, and a little fun to hold. Cash is emotional and intuitive. Cash gets our attention.

You may hold onto the cash. You may deposit cash to the bank. Either way, record cash income as revenue and report it to your accountant. Not only do you want to be safe from the long arm of the law, it's morally the right thing to do. No, I'm not your conscience, but I can't help but point out your office staff can see and will know. What behavior do you want from them?

Shared Budgeting

The first time I presented a talk called Buying Bacon and the simple financial concepts contained in this book, the businesses owners in attendance showed real interest.

Many of those businesses are owned by a married couple or are partnerships between two or more people. In that situation, who is responsible for handling the financial issues? Everyone with an ownership stake. Who does this work? Generally, whoever is nerdiest should build and run the budget.

I didn't mention this important issue during the first talk. A married couple, who owned a business, later came to me with thoughts and questions. One was very excited about all the intricacies. The other looked a little haunted.

One was a nerd, the other a free spirit. The nerd developed a detailed spreadsheet and did all the financial intricacies. The free spirit was thankful for an improved financial situation for their business but had no idea what the nerd was doing. This was likely to develop into a business financial issue and maybe even a marital problem.

I learned how to deal with this issue at FPU and found it to be very accurate in my own home.

Nerds, good news! It's your job to develop the spreadsheet, lay out the categories, and set the budget.

Free spirits, it's your job to review it and then, and this is critical, change something.

Nerds, I know it's hard to let someone touch your work. I get it. Your budget is awesome. Your spreadsheet is meticulous. The numbers all line up. This thing is perfect! But, and this is also very important, if the free spirit doesn't change something, then your finances will get damaged or destroyed by your partner. It's not malicious. They won't mean to, but they won't be on board. They'll make money decisions they are entitled to as owners, but those decisions will work against the budget. Because, look, a butterfly!

You need weigh in to get buy in. When a person reviews and changes something, it becomes theirs as well. They'll then have ownership of the budget. They'll know the budget, understand the real financial limits of your company, and will work with you instead of against, or at least parallel to you.

Free Spirits

Free spirits, it's time to stop skimming.

Some people won't do a budget. No matter how dire the financial situation, no matter how much power a budget provides, they just won't do it. The thought of all those numbers shuts their brain off. A spreadsheet makes them vomit a little in the back of their mouths. Yes, to free spirits, it's that gross.

I don't understand this, but I can accept it.

Free spirits, hear me now. There is no way to ensure winning at small business finances without a budget. None. There is no free lunch.

But there is another way to get close. Don't skim the next two chapters.

Bacon Bits

- Review last month's budget and create next month's budget at a scheduled time after the month ends. Ten to fifteen days after month end will give everyone time to review and reconcile.
- For small shops, consider the 10/25 financial cycle.
- Record all cash payments.
- For businesses with more than one owner, budgeting should be done by the nerd. The free spirit must change something.

Chapter 9: The Top-Line Profit Method
Take what is yours.

"The old, been-around-forever, profitless formula is: Sales – Expenses = Profit. The new, Profit First Formula is: Sales – Profit = Expenses. The math in both formulas is the same. Logically, nothing has changed. But Profit First speaks to human behavior—it accounts for the regular Joes of the world, like me." -Mike Michalowicz

Main-Land was founded by Darryl Brown in 1974. Darryl was a soil scientist and loved everything about land. He was passionate about his clients. He loved his staff and was loyal to a fault. He was extremely smart, personable, and a treasured mentor to many, including myself.

Darryl loved digging holes. He lived on a farm growing up so getting his hands dirty was life for him. He was in his element out in the woods with an auger or excavator, digging holes, and looking for the best soils for his clients' projects. Even though he had a dozen or more employees performing a myriad of engineering, surveying, or scientific tasks back at the office, he was most often out in the field doing what he loved.

He loved people. He loved land. He didn't love computers. He didn't love lists of numbers. He didn't love deeply focusing on a single mental task all day. He could do those things, but he didn't love them.

Darryl successfully operated Main-Land for 38 years. I won't critique how he ran things because he did a great job. Success speaks for itself.

He did, however, critique himself. After I took over the company, we sat down for some important transfer of experience and advice.

When it came to money, he said, "Bob, watch the checkbook. Don't ever miss payroll. Ever. That doesn't go over well. Don't spend too much, either. If there's money in the checkbook, you can deal with everything else. It's like air. If you don't have air, nothing else matters."

"Check," I replied. "Money is vaporous." I can be a little snarky sometimes.

He looked at me. His face smiled, but his eyes did not.

I deserved that.

"When it comes to cash flow, it's a bit of a ride. You might want to budget or something. Check it out. You've got the right mindset for it." Yes, he basically called me a nerd.

Darryl loved being outside. He didn't love budgeting. He chose to forgo some of the office work in order to spend more productive time outside.

As such, Darryl operated with the checkbook method of finances. He had great intuition and judgement. He saw cash flow changes before they happened and adjusted his spending to suit, on the fly. He was good at it and we all rested easy knowing his skill and panache, acquired over decades of experience and hard work, would keep the company running smoothly. And it did.

Do you have decades of experience handling money by intuition, by the checkbook method of financing? Do you have decades of profit to show for all that work?

You want to make a profit. But you abhor the thought of a budget. Are you so in love with what you do that financial planning and operating a budget has never been and will never be a priority for your time?

My job with this book is to provide information and ideas for you to use to operate your company finances profitably. My job isn't to make you do anything. I wouldn't if I could. I have no grand master scheme to take over the world. I'm not giving you permission to skip a budget, but you don't need my permission.

If you have been operating your company on the checkbook method of finances and have too little or no profit to show for it, stick with me. Bacon is coming. If you have never done and will never do a budget, stick with me. Bacon is still coming. There is another way. The top line profit method doesn't provide the additional benefits of a budget, but it can ensure profit if properly performed.

If the last chapters made you roll your eyes and think, "Nuh uh. Good thing I skimmed it because there is no way, never, I will ever do a budget," then the top line profit method may be for you.

I'll never know if Darryl suggested I start using a budget because he thought it was a better way or if he knew I don't have the intuitive chops for mastery of the checkbook method of financing. Maybe he just feared I would fly right off the cash flow rollercoaster.

Darryl passed away in 2016 and is sorely missed. Thank you, Darryl. Thank you for taking care of us, helping all those clients with their land, and all the great times we had as Main-Landers.

Operating on the Fly

Free spirited entrepreneurs are really good at operating on the fly. They can receive information, make decisions, and move forward confidently, all at the speed of a hummingbird on an energy drink. They're not only good at it, they love it! They thrive on the rollercoaster, swim with the ebb and flow, and roll with the punches.

Further, operating on the fly means no one tells them what to do. An entrepreneur decides, in the moment, regardless of who told them what. An entrepreneur is the master of her own destiny, king of his own hill.

Operating on the fly means freedom. Businesspeople operating on the fly have the ultimate freedom to decide what to do in the only moment that matters: right now. If an entrepreneur makes a plan, but decides later to change it, no worries. It's how they roll.

Many entrepreneurs use the checkbook method of finances for these reasons. It's operating business finances on the fly.

Good news, free spirits! The top-line method of finances will let you keep operating on the fly! I promise! Because you are good at it and because you are an investor and an innovator.

Investing and Innovating

Entrepreneurs are great investors. An entrepreneur will quickly and intuitively understand what works and what doesn't. They take their resources and invest in what works. They are so good at this that any resource sitting untapped is a waste.

An unscheduled hour isn't a free moment to rest but an opportunity to get a head start on the next task.

If a company vehicle sits in the lot all day, an entrepreneur wonders what it could be hauling to make it productive. They don't see an unused car; they see an asset sitting idle, making no money.

A dollar in the checkbook is a dollar to invest in the next product, a new marketing idea, or growing the company.

See the problem? No? Keep reading.

Entrepreneurs are also great innovators. Give an entrepreneur an idea, two weeks, and a couple of paperclips and they will find a way to build a company selling a great product across a region. Take the paper clips away and they will innovate their way into expense cutting mode and get by with far less than anyone thought possible.

Entrepreneurs figure out how to get fourteen hours work done in ten.

Entrepreneurs decide to sell the unused vehicle at just the right time to keep the company running.

When there is no money in the checkbook, it's the entrepreneur who innovatively cuts corners, does more with less, and finds a way to make ends meet.

There is no better analogy than The Toothpaste Tube Principle. I learned this from the entrepreneurial expert Mike Michalowicz.

When the toothpaste tube is full, you use a generous dollop. You cover the bristles and curl the ends like a toothpaste commercial. Your mouth foams up like a rabid animal, which prompts you to chase your young children around the house. This irritates your spouse, but at least the kids are wound up and your teeth feel great.

When the toothpaste tube is nearly empty, as defined by any reasonable person calling it totally empty, then you squeeze out a few toothpaste molecules, just enough to freshen your mouth. It might just overpower the taste of white rice.

Either way, your teeth get brushed.

Operating finances on the fly, by the checkbook method of financing, is just like that. Entrepreneurs, especially free spirits, excel at spending money based on how much there is in the tube. Entrepreneurs invest with a generous dollop in times of plenty and innovate to get by on a few dollars in times of need.

"Yeah, bub, so what's the problem?"

I called it, didn't I? That's exactly what you were thinking.

The Problems

Being really good at business requires a metric ton of experience, character, and wisdom, to name just a few. If you want to ensure profit from business, then you need to be perfect at business.

Are you perfect?

Careful. I know your spouse's answer to this question.

There are problems all businesspeople experience, which will impact your ability to keep profit.

Relaxing the Grip on Finances

A hummingbird will zip through the forest, unerringly avoiding branches, leaves, and the occasional lurking spider. To do so, not only must it see those obstacles, it must have an intuitive understanding of those problems. It must have a good gut, which is where the analogy breaks down. There is no such thing as a fat hummingbird.

On what do you base your financial gut? Clearly, a businessperson must spend time in the checkbook to use the checkbook method of financing. It will provide a high-level understanding of the finances.

The other way to get into the numbers on a deeper level is to reconcile the account. You do reconcile your accounts, right? Reconcile every month to stay on top of the numbers. It is, at best, looking backward only a month.

Reconciling is not looking ahead. You have your flawless gut for that.

If at any point your intuitive understanding of the finances is lost, even for just a few days, mistakes will be made, money will be spent, and little to none will be left for profit. Good luck taking a vacation.

Red Alert

Many entrepreneurs won't operate with much of a checkbook buffer because they end up investing the extra cash. It means a checkbook can go from flush to empty in a very short amount of time. There's little warning. There's a red rectangle in the wall which starts blinking and a siren wails. Red alert! Red alert!

So, when a business runs out of money, the owner goes into beast mode to sell product, sell assets, and juggle money and tasks, praying they really are a miracle worker.

Why the beast mode? Why the panic? Because innovation takes time to design and implement. The owner knows this and jumps quickly. I did, too, but not anymore when I can help it. I have eaten too much over the years to jump much.

Operating at red alert is quite possible and may even be fun for some. However, it is not efficient. Say goodbye to profit.

The Rollercoaster

Entrepreneurs love to ride the financial rollercoaster. They work the hills and the valleys. They invest on the hills and innovate in the valleys. It's part of who they are.

Why are they at red alert in the valleys? *Because* they invest on the hills.

While the nerds are budgeting for their investments to buy at the right moment, free spirits just do it when they are up on the hill. It's an *investment.* How much do free spirits invest? All of it. Every last available dollar. They invest as much as they can to get the biggest bang for their buck. I'm not here to tell you they're wrong. Even if they are.

Worse, the rollercoaster is unpredictable.

Free spirits, do you remember the wavy rollercoaster cashflow chart back in Chapter 3? Go back and look. The chart zigged up and zagged down like a lifetime chainsaw logger signing a check. The problem with the chart is, wait for it, I made it up. Yep. Sorry about that. It's totally fictional. While it's representative of a typical cash cycle, it won't be your cash cycle this year. This year's cycle won't look like next years. You understand.

Unless years are spent budgeting and tracking these things, there's little pattern to find and use. Without a pattern, deciding when to invest is difficult.

Once again, you must rely on your perfect gut.

If the businessperson fails in this, then the investment won't be well utilized, growth may be stymied, and the red alerts will get worse. Again, profit takes a back seat to survival.

Survive and Thrive

Donald Miller, in his book, *Building a Storybrand*, makes the case that people's brains are, by default, always looking to survive and thrive. Our brains will survive first and thrive second. We don't even know our three pounds of grey matter is spinning all the time. We can't stop it even if we knew.

Free spirited entrepreneurs take this a step further. From a business perspective, they operate on survive and thrive all the time. On the hills of the rollercoaster, they thrive. In the valleys, they survive.

And they are very good at it.

That's the point. That's their problem. Free spirited entrepreneurs struggle to take a timeout, press pause, and systematize a better way.

As a result, there's none or not enough profit.

I want you to have profit. Real profit. Cash-in-the-bank profit. Bacon buying profit.

Top-Line

So, take your profit before you spend anything.

The top-line method of finances is simply taking money out of your checkbook before you spend the rest on your business.

It sounds too simple. Good news: it is that simple and easy to systematize, too. Read on.

Bacon Bits

- If you won't budget, then the best you can do to understand your finances is keeping your checkbook up to date and reconciling: the checkbook method of financing.
- If you won't budget, you must ride the money mood cycle rollercoaster, investing on the peaks, innovating in the valleys.
- No matter how good you are at this, there are unavoidable problems. Profit takes a hit.
- Secure profit before you spend on expenses.

Chapter 10: Systematize Profit First
Make it simple and easy to do.

"The cost of inaction is greater than the cost of making a mistake." – Carla Harris

"Learning new systems and processes is not mandatory...but neither is staying in business." — Bobby Darnell

I had been running Main-Land for a couple of months when I was first approached by an employee about a training seminar request.

"I need to take two days next week for a seminar on performing a feline attitudectomy. Can I go Thursday through Friday? And I get paid for that, right? Don't worry about overnight; I'll stay at my sister's."

I replied with a raised eyebrow, "Uh, attituduhwhat? Well, it sounds important. Approved."

Then, a week later, another person asked, "There's this class about Canine Ballicker Syndrome. I think maybe my dog has it. The local vet clinic is teaching about it, at a great price. Can I have Tuesday to go, and I'll bring back all the notes and diagrams."

"Well…" I hesitated, questioning my firm belief that dogs are better than cats. "If you think you should really go."

I wish those were real classes. I spared you from thinking about things like soil horizons classification and stormwater phosphorus concentrations. We really love land here at Main-Land.

The point is every time an issue came up, I had to make a decision, immediately and correctly, and communicate it clearly. If money was great and I was in a good mood, then we would go learn about life-saving feline attitudectomies. If not, then the dog would go on… doing what dogs do.

Before long, I systematized training requests. If the class is work related, technical, less than X dollars, and one day or less long, then just get supervisor approval and go. Anything more, let me know. A little while later, I systematized it further by stipulating a Y dollar cap and two-day limit with CAO approval. We put in minimums and maximums to the number of days per year spent training without approval. We provided lists of recommended classes.

We systematized the process, because it's what entrepreneurs do to delegate and build efficiencies.

What Is Needed

To use the Top-Line Method of Finances as a system, you'll need two things:

1. a separate savings account at your local community bank, and
2. a calculator, if you are bad at fifth grade math.

That's not too bad, is it?

At the bank, create another savings account. Seriously, they don't seem to mind how many separate accounts you have. If they do, try a smaller community bank where you can walk in and talk to a decision maker. Ask for an additional savings account. Some banks even allow account creation online for existing customers.

Name the account. You can call it "Muskrat" if you want, but I will respectfully suggest "Profit Savings Account."

The account can be a simple savings account. The interest rate doesn't matter. If you can get check writing privileges with this account for free, great. Otherwise, don't. The profit account is a temporary holding place to transfer money in and out.

As for a calculator, my elementary school teacher was wrong. We do, in fact, carry a calculator with us all the time. They're made by LG, Samsung, or maybe Apple.

The System

Keeping profit should be easy. Let's create a system for the Top-Line Method of Finances, step by step.

Step 1: Make the Deposit

Payments for your work keep coming in the mail. Let's pray they never stop.

Some businesspeople run to the bank and make deposits every day. Some run to the bank only when the checkbook register bottoms out. Some don't run at all, but make deposits electronically, which is handy and techno-cool. Regardless, deposits of a known total are made.

Go make the deposit to the checking account, just like you always have.

Step 2: Figure Profit

As soon as you can, or even in advance, figure a percentage of the deposit that will be the profit. Let's make the profit 10%, to keep the math easy. Figure how much 10% of the deposit was. If fifth grade math is a problem, no worries. Use a calculator app on your phone. I'm not looking.

Step 3: Move the Profit

As soon as you can, view your bank account online. Use your computer or the app on your phone. I'm getting older so the smaller text on my phone is getting harder to read, so I tend to use the computer.

Use the online tools to transfer the profit amount from the checking account to the profit savings account.

Timing

Timing is important here.

No one is going to come take your money. The bank won't move it around on you. There's no slow-burn fuse to a bomb on the vault door.

Timing is important because of you.

Do all of the steps on the same day. Do it within the same hour as long as the deposit has shown up in the account. If you wait until the next day, then it becomes the next day, then next week, then it has been spent. By you.

A better-timed plan is to split the money at the time of deposit. If you are respectful and friendly to the tellers, they may even give you a lollipop. The only reason I suggest splitting off profit electronically afterward is to force you to spend time looking at your accounts in real time, online. If you have more than one additional account, you'll be well advised to keep an eye on them. You are fully warned.

What's Left

You moved (or split at time of deposit) 10% of your money to the profit account. Some quick math shows you still have 90% of your money to use as you see fit, through the checkbook method of financing. I did promise not to take it away, didn't I? When the toothpaste tube – aka checkbook register – is nearly empty, innovate to cut corners with the dollars you have left. But this time, do it stress free because you *already took out your profit.*

What you do with the money in the profit account is the subject of the next chapter.

How Much Profit

My mother's uncle, Donald, was a civil engineer in Connecticut. Shortly after I purchased Main-Land, he was visiting Maine when we had a bit of a family reunion at my parents' house in Embden.

My great Uncle Don, who hadn't talked to me about business even once in the past, cornered me on the front deck to bring up the subject of profit. He hooked his thumbs in the suspenders he wore over his pinstriped shirt and spoke with a grin.

"How much profit you get?" He looked me straight in the eyes. His were clear, blue, and sharp. Mine were wide open and horrified.

"Uh, excuse me?" I stammered. "Profit?"

"Yeah, profit? How much you get? Do you have a number?"

"I'm sure there's a number. Twelve. Twelve sounds like a good number." I had no idea what the number really was.

His gaze pierced my brain. But he smiled jovially.

"My partner at my old firm used to say, 'You should take just as much profit as you can get. I say that's not right. What do you say?"

"Muskrat. I don't know. I'm a capitalist at heart, so, as much as I can get?" It was clearly a question.

"What if they can't afford you?" he asked back.

"I dunno."

"What if it's a town who's hired you? Isn't that taxpayer money?"

"I dunno," I replied, even lamer, if that were possible.

"Think you should figure it all out?" he asked, his eyebrows almost reaching a non-existent hairline and those blue eyes flashing, bemused.

Relieved to get a question I could answer, I said, "Yep. I've got some thinking to do."

He handed me a cold beer off the sidebar and grinned. It was the most awkward and important business conversation I ever experienced. If he was still alive, I would bring him beer so he could ask me more questions.

In the last section, we used 10% as a profit number for the Top-Line Method. Ten percent is a nice round number, making the math more of a fourth-grade level. Did the idea of operating your business at only 90% make you pucker a little bit? Did 10% seem like a lot?

How much profit should you take?

Well, it depends.

First, ease into the Top-Line Method. Consider starting at 1% or 2%. It may not be a lot of money, but you can always increase it incrementally over the coming months until you are comfortable.

Next, there are client standards. Some clients want your product and will live with paying 15% or 20% profit, or even more. Others require a much smaller profit margin. For example, many state and federal authorities require an overhead audit and billing procedures disclosing and setting your profit margin. Maine DOT, for example, likes to see and may stipulate 8% or less.

If you suffer seasonality, off-season profit margins may be small or even zero. At peak season, the business will then increase profit percentages to cover. For example, if you make

5% profit for three months and 10% for six months, then 15% during peak season may be very reasonable.

Practically, consider the general business practices in a free economy. Most people will compete happily at 10% profit. If your whole market is duking it out at 10%, what will happen to your business if you take 15%? A profit margin over 10% is difficult to maintain competitively in many industries. Your industry may be different, so adjust accordingly.

Finally, know your own morality. Profit is not a four-letter word. It's okay to make as much profit as you can. It's not okay to do it while violating your own ethical standards. Know what you will and will not do to make profit. Know from whom you will and will not earn a profit. Know it in your heart, so when the opportunity comes to increase profit, you will know when to say no without hesitation.

Again, Taxes Suck

By now, you know how I feel about taxes. Really, my beef isn't with the idea of taxes. I want at least some of the things the government provides. My beef is really about how the government wastes so much of my taxes. As a society, we could send half tax payments and be just fine. This is my humble opinion, which counts because this is my book.

Maybe you're more altruistic. Maybe you like paying your taxes. Cool. Please do.

Like it or not, skipping taxes is a pipe dream. Taxes must be paid. If you don't, you will quickly see how the government spends your tax dollars on prisons.

So, pay your taxes. It's mandatory.

Like your profit account, open another account for taxes. You can name it whatever you want, but I use "tax savings account."

In the next chapter, we will discuss what to do with the money in the profit account. One of those things will be to set aside money for taxes.

How much taxes need to be set aside depends on where you live and what you do for a living. It varies widely.

To keep things simple, you can back into a tax savings percentage. Say your accountant suggests you will have about $60,000 for taxes this year, paid quarterly. You know you are a $1,000,000 company, so you will need to save a tax percentage of about 6% of revenue. In this example, every deposit will get split as: 10% to the profit account, 6% to the tax savings account, and 84% to the checking account.

More on taxes later.

Optional: CERA

Those nerds. They think they're so smart. They save up all year to buy big capital purchases. They pay with cash when the equipment is on sale, even if their business is in a cash valley. They have it all figured out.

The joke's on them.

Free spirits, you can use the Top-Line Method of Finances to save up for big purchases, too.

Dealing with CERA is a little different from using percentages for profit or taxes. CERA saving uses a set dollar figure. Use the steps below.

1. Create a CERA account, just like profit or tax savings.
2. Figure out what you want to save up to buy. For Main-Land, we use CERA for computers, survey equipment, cars, and expensive suites of technical software. For Bob's Bacon Bistro, it was a $16,000 bacon stretcher. Whatever you decide to buy that year, add it to a list, and then total up how much money you will probably need. No idea what you will buy? Take a stab at what you want for the purchasing opportunity, when it arrives, and use that figure. It's better than the money mood cycle.
3. Estimate the number of times you will do a deposit. If you use the 10/25 principle, then you make deposits 24 times a year. If you go twice a week, then you make deposits 104 times a year.
4. Divide the total annual amount on big capital expenditures by the number of deposits you will make. For example, if Bob needs to buy a $16,000 bacon stretcher and Bob will make 52 deposits this year, then

the CERA account will need $16k / 52 = $308 each deposit.

5. Every time a deposit is made, transfer the CERA deposit amount to the CERA account. By the end of the year, CERA will have the money you need.

If you need it sooner than year-end, then do the math and figure out how many deposits will be made before you need to make your purchase.

If things are super tight and you skip a CERA deposit, double up next time.

There is power in buying with cash. There is savings to buying off-season or when a good deal crops up. Consider saving up in the CERA account to be ready instead of hoping to do it when cashflow is on a hilltop.

Impulse Control

By now, you have multiple accounts: Checking, savings, profit, tax, and CERA.

Nerds go look at those accounts often. They measure the accounts, track their progress, graph the trends, and generally fret over the appropriateness of their financial system.

Free spirits just see money not being used, especially when in a cashflow valley.

When we see something shiny, we've got to have it. New car? I can afford it. Was that my buddy on a motorcycle? He's a dirty rat. Now I want a motorcycle. Most nefarious are shiny things for the business, like a new sign, high-end technology, or office accoutrements. Shiny business expenses are easy to rationalize.

For some people, a stash of money is a significant temptation. Set up a system to protect yourself from you.

A second bank without check-writing or debit card privileges will do the job. To get the money out, you will have to go there in person. Geographically separate accounts will remove most impulsive temptations.

Another option is to use double signatures. You can buy checks requiring two signatures instead of the more typical one signature. Then when you want something out of an account, you need sign-off by a person you designate to hold you accountable.

If you have a real problem with this issue, do both. Create a system to control your own behavior. That's how you win.

Profit First

Much of the Top-Line Method of Finances is also described by Mike Michalowicz in his book *Profit First*. Mike gives lots of information about income, percentages, taxes, and other intricacies of this method. For any free-spirited entrepreneur using this method, *Profit First* is a must read. I mean it. Go buy the book right now. But finish this one first.

Bacon Bits

- Go to your local community bank and open a new savings account for profit.
- Decide how much your profit percentage should be.
- At time of normal deposits, or immediately thereafter, transfer your profit percentage into your profit account.
- Consider doing this for taxes as well.
- Consider doing this to save for large expenses as well.
- If you have trouble with self-control, consider opening these accounts, without checks or debit cards, at a different bank.

Chapter 11: What to Do with Profit
Buy bacon, of course.

"By failing to prepare, you are preparing to fail." - Benjamin Franklin

"... do not set your heart on what you will eat or drink; do not worry about it. For the pagan world runs after all such things, and your Father knows that you need them. But seek his kingdom, and these things will be given to you as well." - Luke 12:29-31

"**B**oys, listen up. I've got something to talk about."

As a parent, car time is a great time to talk to kids. Parents are in the driver's seat and it's a well-known law of automobiles: the driver controls the radio. No radio means the parent's voice is all those little darling spawn can hear.

When one has three teenage sons trapped in the car, the opportunity is not to be missed.

"Dad, not this again," whined one knob-kneed kid.

"No pontification," hissed another through his braces.

"The driver makes the rules," I quipped happily, which turned against me later when they got their learner's permits.

I continued. "There are two kinds of people in the world: earners and takers.

"Some people earn their way through life. They build. They invent. They create. They work with their hands and their brains to add value to their organization and society as a whole. And they're paid to do so. We're designed to work.

"Other people are takers. Some go through life feeling like everyone is against them. The world can be harsh, and maybe they've had a full steaming bowlful of nasty. Some are desperate and will take anything to survive. Some are cynical and feel like the world owes them a break. A few takers were given easy lives and expect it to continue even when their money runs out. Regardless of the reason, takers end up with what others have earned."

I looked in the rear-view mirror just in time to catch an eye-roll.

"Look, guys. This is important. Why do you think your mom and I make you work around the house? Why did we leave the dishwasher broken? Why did I teach you to swing a maul? Why do we have a push mower instead of a zero-turn? Do you think we can't afford it?"

"No," one answered, forlorn.

"A riding mower was an option?" asked another.

"Ha! Not until you all move out. Listen, would you rather be an earner or a taker?"

"Earner," they all answered in monotone unison. I may have given this pontification before. But this time, I had a trick up my sleeve.

"Why?" I asked.

All went silent as they mulled over this turn of events.

After a few moments, one said, "So we can have nice stuff." A future capitalist was just made.

"No," I answered. "Though, that's a nice perquisite."

My youngest piped up, "What's perkiest?"

"Perquisite. Perk. Um, it's a privilege you get for earning. If you make money, you can buy stuff. If you don't make money, you can't buy stuff."

"So, why be an earner?" I repeated. More silence, stretching on for long moments.

Another answer came, slowly and as more of a question. "To help people?"

"Bingo!"

I caught a metal-filled grin in the mirror.

I continued, "Look, God made you for many good purposes. One of the most important is to help people. And you cannot give…"

"…what you don't have," my oldest finished.

"That's right. You cannot give what you don't have. Unless you're in Congress."

The eye-roll this time came from my wife, but she had one of those little quirky grins I find adorable.

From the backseat, another kid opined, "That's not right. The government gives only what they take." And a future libertarian was just made.

"Truth," I affirmed. "Earners make their way through life. And most give as they go. Takers, whether or not they need to be, slide through life on what they are given. They have trouble giving because they don't have much. And what they have has little value to them because they didn't earn it. Get it?"

A chorus of obligatory "yups" and "yeahs" followed. But they spent the rest of the ride staring quietly out the windows, lost in their thoughts.

Parenting is a series of teachable moments that always end with, "Am I getting through to them?" I should ask my folks when it ends. I suspect I know the answer.

As a business owner, you are a supreme earner. You build. You invent. You create. You add lots of value to your community. And you should be paid for it.

Profit isn't a four-letter word. All too often people today use the word as a curse. Profit is payment made for your risk and the value you add. You earned it. You didn't take it.

Let us earn some profit. With profit, we can help people even more.

A Plan for Profit

A financial concept has become popular today on college campuses. For someone to get rich someone else becomes poor. If your slice of the pie becomes larger, someone else's slice must become smaller. This is total malarkey. It's a lie told by takers and bought hook, line, and sinker by other takers.

Mmmm, pie. Great. Now I'm full-on hangry. I want pie.

The economy isn't a pie. The economy is a bonfire. More fuel on the bonfire will make the bonfire bigger and hotter! Your effort and the resulting business product are more fuel. Everyone is warmed by it.

The profit from your business is your just rewards for your fuel. You worked hard and risked much for this profit. You have earned it.

No one suffered so you may have profit, despite all those movies you saw. Sorry, they lie in movies. When you sold your product to a customer, you met the customer's need. You didn't take anything from them. You helped them with your product, and they paid you for the help. You didn't take it from anyone. You cannot force anyone to buy your product because you're not Congress.

You have *earned* your profit by growing the free market.

If you use a budget and properly handle your successful business's cash flow as outlined so far in this book, profit has been deposited into the best bank account of all: the profit savings account. Don't feel guilty about it. You made profit by helping meet the needs of others.

By this point, you know you need a plan for profit just as much as your cash flow. If you have no plan for your profit, you'll end up with a big boat, a fast car, and no bacon. At home, you'll hurt your family. At work, it gets worse. You'll hurt many families.

What you do with your profit is up to you. I didn't earn it, it's not mine, and so who am I to say what you do with your profits?

But I have some ideas.

Taxes

Before we can get into handling profit, we need to talk about taxes. Again. I know this will shock you, but profit is taxable. That's right. Uncle Sam has his fingers in every pocket, even the little mystery pocket in your jeans.

Before profit is spent, take out the taxes and set it aside in your tax savings account. What's left is net profit for you.

How much to take out for income taxes is the subject of many accounting books and large sections of the IRS tax code.

In Maine, income taxes for federal and state combined will be between 30% and 35% of profit. Some states, where I would live if I didn't love it here, don't have state income taxes at all. Business nirvana.

Email your accountant, explain you're setting aside taxes for profit, and ask what rough percentage to use for federal and state income taxes. They may say, "It depends," and they'd be right. But ask for a rough number.

The new federal tax code is nice to engineers, so I set this number at the low end of the Maine range. I use 21% for federal (yours will vary depending on your type and structure of business) and 8% for Maine. Then I bump it up a tad, just because surprises make me grumpy. I use 30%.

For now, just get as close as you can, with your accountant's help. We'll be coming back to this once a plan is made for net profit.

Percentage Profit Split Method

Every month, after reconciling the accounts, transferring CERA, transferring income taxes, and transferring profit, split the net profit according to predetermined percentages to profit categories.

Six categories are suggested below.

Charitable Giving

Giving is actually good for business. Here's how it works.

Business is all about transactions for goods or services. People buy goods and services from companies they trust. Trust is a necessary part of any transaction. The purchaser must trust the product they buy will produce the result promised by the seller.

Lack of trust increases risk, and risk has a cost. Consider the last time you bought a used car. You wanted the best deal you could get for the best car you could afford. If you had questions about the character of the seller, the price goes down in your mind, right? How do you know if the car has some problem that will manifest two days after the 30-day warranty? If you trust the seller, you know you can trust the car. You'll pay closer to asking price.

Did you catch that word? Character.

To have trust in the product, you want to know the character of the seller. Big companies spend gobs of money marketing their good character. You see it every day on television and online.

As the owner, your character is key. Your entire company and all of your staff will follow your character. The success of your business hinges directly on your character. Your character is of prime importance to making profitable sales.

There are many ways to build your character, including pain, education, and experience. That said, there's no better way to build character than to give.

Giving changes a person's heart. Giving improves character. And it's super fun.

God knows this. He instructs His people to give, starting at 10% of personal income, known as the tithe in church circles.

Here's the thing: God doesn't need your money. He owns everything, anyway. The tithe isn't about supporting the church. If you don't give, He'll find a way to fund His church. As if the omnipotent creator of everything needs your financial help.

Tithing is about your heart. When a person gives, it changes them. Their life perspective shifts. They gain character. Giving is about character building.

So, giving builds character. Character builds trust. Trust builds your business. It's really simple. So, please consider giving.

How much you give and to whom is up to you.

Everyone has many passions in life. Your business is only one. There are many others. Decide which of those passions deserve your giving. Then cut them a check according to the pre-determined percentage.

For small business owners, these funds are rather limited. Be discerning. Your small business cannot contribute to every charitable cause knocking on your door. If you did, the amount would be so small you would barely help any of them. Make your charitable dollars count by giving most of your charity to one or two causes.

Giving of your time is even better. For business owners, time is often more valuable than cash. Give your time to non-profits for which you have passion.

Personally, I'm passionate about those middle schoolers. I donate many hours to them. I'm also passionate about economic development and give many hours to local Chambers of Commerce and other groups. Maybe you are more passionate about the poor, or the elderly, or the environment. Give your time where you see fit.

And, of course, giving time is also good for business. Time spent volunteering causes you to rub elbows, shoulder to shoulder, with people just like you. You become friends with them. When they hear of a need your business provides, you know who they'll recommend.

Charitable giving is first on this list for a reason. Giving is that important.

Owner Profit

Lest you think you'll give all your profit away, here is where I disabuse you of the notion.

Who takes on the risk of business? Who takes on the business lifestyle which dictates long hours? Who wakes up at three in the morning and thinks about marketing strategies and operational improvements? Who wears the responsibility for all those families depending on a fruitful career?

You do.

The profit is yours. Take some home. Transfer the pre-determined percentage of profit directly into your personal checking account.

Too many small business owners leave nothing for themselves. Every penny is rolled back into the business, especially for startups.

Instead, take some home, even if you set your owner profit percentage to only 1%. It may only buy a dinner with your spouse. Do it anyway. Even small celebrations show your family and yourself the trials of business have their rewards.

If you have big profit, then buy the big boat.

The IRS would demand I caution you about hiding these transfers, if I cared about their feelings. The transfer to your personal account is an owner disbursement. It is taxable (more on that later). Enter this disbursement, as with all other transfers, directly into the checkbook register, where it can be easily found by you, your accountant, and the IRS auditor.

Profit Sharing

"You know where bonuses come from, don't you? They come from Bonusland."

Years ago, I attended a business seminar series called Entreleadership in Nashville, Tennessee. I highly recommend it as the best money spent on business training. The speaker was Chris Hogan, a talented author, podcast host, and financial coach to nationally known professional athletes. Chris was teaching on the differences between bonuses and profit sharing.

> Nerd alert. I did the math. For my company, Entreleadership Master Series paid for itself in 13 days. I highly recommend it as the best money spent on training.
>
> I was not paid to say this, but I will anyway. Visit them at www.entreleadership.com

A bonus is a gift for a job well done.

The bonus is good. Budget for bonuses in the OpEx category and give them away as you see fit. Unfortunately, this depends on a benevolent dictator: you. You giveth and you taketh away.

Do you see it this way? No! You see the bonus as earned by the team members. The problem is your team members don't understand the intricate finances of your company. Nor should most of them. But because they don't understand your company finances, they see it as a gift from someone who loves and appreciates them. They may or may not see it as directly correlating to their performance, to say nothing about a specific key performance indicator. No, the bonus comes from Bonusland.

Profit sharing is something different. Profit sharing is giving your team a pre-determined percentage of the profits. The better each team member performs, the more money they will receive in reward. If they help to make the profit, they will reap some back as a reward. Profit sharing turns employees into partners in your mission. They start to perform like owners. Once they start to act like owners, your business will skyrocket.

Profit sharing is tricky.

Profit sharing needs to be divided up fairly between each team member. There are many considerations here, including responsibility and salary, hours worked, deals closed, projects managed, accounts handled, contributed revenue, seniority, position and title, meeting goals, and many others, which vary from business to business. Which of these do you use as performance indicators to determine how to split the profit sharing? Once determined, these metrics should be transparent to each team member, so they see how their day to day actions affect the profit.

It gets harder. There are many metrics which affect profit. The temptation will be to include them all. I went that route initially. Main-Land's staff are some of the brightest people I know. They are seriously smart. Yet, most found all those metrics to be too much to understand. Many Main-Landers gave up and just did their job as best they could, as they always do. I failed to use profit as a motivator.

It gets harder still. Profit sharing must be set up so each team member can personally and directly affect the metrics it is based upon.

For example, say your business is a service business with revenue earned based solely on billable hours. It makes sense to base the profit sharing on a billable hours metric. If a team member bills more hours than a certain threshold, their profit sharing metric increases. This would work for many of your staff, unless, of course, when and where they work is controlled by a supervisor. In that common case, profit sharing is nothing more than a bonus and fails to produce the motivation sought. If a person cannot affect the metric, they won't be motivated to improve it.

Keep profit sharing simple. Target the one or two metrics which help the business most *and* the team members can personally and directly affect. This may mean different parts of your team have different profit sharing schemes, which will be complicated for you but easy for them.

The best profit sharing metrics will motivate teams to help each other win. In the above example, for staff billing hours, maybe the best metric is days without errors, since errors require costly rework. But for those staff who control their own time, billable hours may be the right metric. Then for the project manager who depends on those people performing like owners, project profitability may be the best metric. Each team member improving their metric then boosts the whole team's win.

If you decide to try profit sharing, remember you are the owner and you are in charge. Promise them at implementation it will change, because it will. Profit sharing takes a lot of trial and error to get right. Also promise them you won't change it without being transparent about the changes before the metrics take effect, so they have time to adjust.

Bonuses are good. Budget for bonuses and award them when you feel appropriate.

Profit sharing is better because it improves staff motivation. Just be prepared for the work involved to track, report, and adjust the metrics.

Every month transfer the profit sharing percentage to a separate profit sharing savings account. Once the transfer happens, it's no longer your money, so hands off.

We initially wanted to cut profit sharing checks monthly in order to maximize motivation, but our cash flow is far too variable to be correlated to a month's work effort by individuals. Instead, we decided to cut the checks quarterly. Later, we changed to annually because it was requested by the overwhelming majority of our staff. We still report it – in writing - quarterly so they can see how much they have earned in profit sharing.

Extra Business Debt Payments

If your business can stay out of debt, do it. Debt will slow your company growth and is a risk multiplier for your business longevity. Debt will be covered in more depth in the next chapter.

The reality is most businesses have some debt. If you do, one of your goals should be to lessen and eventually eliminate it.

Regular minimum debt payments are handled as part of your budget, in the financial category as discussed earlier.

To pay off your debts as soon as possible, make extra debt payments from a pre-determined percentage of your profits. Even small additional payments to your debt principle will result in significant interest saved and a debt free life sooner.

Debt free life is cool.

Tank Savings

If you think tank savings means saving up for an M1 Abrams main battle tank, you're wrong. But I like the way you think.

Instead, imagine a country boy's pickup truck, jacked and stacked. It has an American flag waiving in the bed. The gas pedal is either at idle or pressed to the mat. There is no in between. The wheels spray gravel everywhere. It's an awesome truck.

Now imagine the truck with a gas tank the size of a teacup.

Seeing the truck sitting on the side of the road is pretty easy to imagine now, right? Too bad it didn't have a sizable auxiliary tank full of gas.

This is a silly analogy, I'll admit, even if I still want that truck. Yet, this is exactly what operating a business is like. Your business is a high performing road warrior truck needing gas to get from gas station to gas station. A teacup of gas isn't going to cut it. You need an auxiliary tank full of gas for when you run out.

Remember the cash flow rollercoaster and the money mood cycle? As if you could forget.

Having some operating cash reserves, or buffer in your checkbook, is critical to weathering the week to week fluctuations. Maintain whatever buffer is right for your business.

But what if you have a bad month? Two bad months? What if your business is seasonal? If your business has enough bad months in a row, the buffer is gone. This leads to door-locking, end-of-business problems.

Remember the story in the first chapter? I had run out of money and payroll was due. I wished I had an account filled with money as a backup to bad times. I wished I had a fuel tank to get me to the next gas station.

Tank Savings is money you set aside for those rainy days. It's an emergency fund for your business. It's an extra fuel tank for the long road of business.

The problem with tank savings is the money just sits there. Oh, it will earn a little interest to maybe keep up with inflation. But the money isn't invested. It's not growing your company. It's not furthering your mission.

The return on investment of tank savings is sleep. Stress is the enemy of sleep. When the checkbook balance gets low and payroll is looming, stress seizes you in a vice and insomnia becomes your mortal enemy. A tank savings account lowers stress, deepens sleep, and allows you to focus on what you do best: your business.

Financial stress is a business killer. It dampens positivity, reduces generosity, and focuses you on getting paid for previous work instead of going out to get more work.

Tank savings will strengthen your business, not slow it down.

Each month transfer your pre-determined percentage to a separate tank savings account, and then just let it sit there. A money market account will increase yield, but avoid certificates of deposit, savings bonds, or any other investment which keeps the money inaccessible for any time period. Tank savings must remain liquid so you can tap it when bad things happen.

How much tank savings you set aside is up to you. Seasonal businesses will want enough to weather their down times as a good start. Having three months of expenses saved is my goal. However, three months may never be attainable for growing companies. Your growth may outpace your savings.

Reaching the point of having enough tank savings to comfortably operate without fear is the goal. If you ever reach it, great job! Slow or stop tank savings at that point.

One last thought on tank savings. Most businesses use a credit line as an emergency fund. When I had no tank savings, the credit line was critically important. As tank savings grew, I used the credit line less and less. Eventually, it can be closed. A credit line is a credit card without the card.

UFO

Do you like to yard sale? Or maybe it's your spouse who must stop at every roadside rummage sale. I'm not into it. I have enough junk. I don't need yours.

Then again, occasionally, you find a gold nugget. It's not on a table or in a cardboard box. It's a small sign by the swing set, reading, "Old commercial fridge, ask to see in basement." It's the "For Sale" sign in the window of the van parked over by the garage. It's the display case housing all the junk for sale.

The above profit splits are optional. It's your profit. Do what you want. This sixth one is even more optional, and maybe better left until you're debt free or have plenty of tank savings. Then again, if you're a highly motivated deal hunter, this may be just your thing.

Open a separate opportunities savings account. Maybe call it your Unspent For Opportunities account.

UFO money can be used to take advantage of a good deal, like your competitor's equipment when he goes out of business or the used van that's perfect for deliveries. Those deals are out there, unknown until you stumble upon them.

The power of cash in a transaction is undeniable. UFO money allows a quick run to the bank for actual green cash. When you show people cash, an immediacy enters the negotiation, which says you're ready to do this deal, right now. It may result in a better price. A credit card or a loan note doesn't have the same effect.

I sometimes struggle with apprehension and guilt if I find a deal I want but know I can't afford. A UFO account takes guilt away, because I set the money aside specifically for this situation.

How much you save in a UFO account is up to you. It will likely depend on the scope and type of your business.

UFO's are real and tangible, if you set aside the money ahead of time.

Budget Profit Split

I use the Percentage Profit Split method because I like to know each of those categories are getting funded. They're all important to me.

There is another way: budget and prioritize them.

Create a mini-budget for your profit. Put the most important categories at the top and the least important at the bottom. When there is profit to split, transfer the amount prescribed from the top to the bottom. When the profit runs out, the transfers stop.

Bob's Bacon Bistro uses this method. Back in chapter six, Bob's budget planned for a profit of $24,000 annually. First, Bob removes taxes. Say Bob removes 21%, which is $5,040. So, Bob budgets his net profit of $24,000 - $5,040 = $18,960 into the following categories.

Category	$	Monthly	Jan	Feb
Charitable Giving	$1,800	$150	$-	$300
Profit Sharing	$3,600	$300	$-	$600
Tank Savings	$3,100	$258	$-	$517
Owner Profit	$3,600	$300	$-	$600
Extra Business Debt Payments	$5,860	$488	$-	$648
UFO	$1,000	$83	$-	$-
Total:	$18,960	$1,580	$-	$2,665

First, notice the category rows have been reordered. This order won't be your order, so you should reorder them to suit you.

The first dollar column is the annual profit budget, decided as Bob saw fit.

Note, this method does mess with profit sharing as a motivator because there is nothing staff can do to increase it. It's a set budget. To combat this, consider splitting profit above the annual profit budget with staff at some predetermined ratio.

The monthly column is simply each annual profit amount divided by twelve.

This chart shows January and February tracking for the sake of the example. For the Bob's Bacon Bistro example, January had no profit, but February had $3,374. After 21% income taxes, that's $2,665.

Profit was split by transferring the amount owed (in this case, for two months) from the top down. The first four categories were fully funded. But notice the business debt category wasn't fully funded. He paid $648 to debt that month and none to UFO.

No worries, though. Bob will sell more bacon in March. We Mainers pack on a few extra pounds when the snow gets deep.

Taxes

Time to return to taxes. You can see from the above example there's a big difference between setting aside 30% and 21% for income taxes. Knowing the rough number is important.

As it turns out, not all your profit is taxable, depending on what you do with it.

Charitable giving is clearly not taxable, with some vague and subjective exceptions controlled by the IRS. Giving to your spouse is mighty sweet but typically not charitable. Nice try.

Profit sharing is basically additional payroll to your staff. Payroll has its own taxes but isn't taxable to you as income.

When calculating how much to set aside for taxes, include owner profit, extra business debt payments, and tank savings. Include UFO if you don't intend to spend it this calendar year.

Calculate this tax percentage to set aside by multiplying the standard income tax rate (for my business in Maine, 30%) by the percentage of your profit that's taxable.

As an example, (no, these aren't my profit split percentages) maybe you set your percentages as follows:

Category	%	Apply
Charitable Giving	10%	
Owner Profit	30%	30%
Profit Sharing	10%	
Extra Business Debt Payments	25%	25%
Tank Savings	15%	15%
UFO	10%	
Total:	100%	70%

Great. Another spreadsheet.

If you use the budget profit split method, don't panic. Just do the math to figure out your category percentages after the fact. For example, $1000 in budgeted charitable giving is 10% of a $10,000 profit budget. Do this for all your profit categories and enter the percentages into the spreadsheet, like above.

If you use the percentage profit split method, then you already have percentages. It's how it works.

These profit split categories in the example spreadsheet above are split by the percentage shown. Some of those categories are taxable. The taxable items have the same percent copied into the Apply column. Adding up the Apply column tells how much of the profit is taxable. In this example, 70% of the profit is taxable.

This exercise results in how much the income tax percentage on profit can be reduced. In this example, the 30% set aside for state and federal income taxes on profit can be reduced to 30% x 70% = 21%.

Regarding the UFO category, it's only taxable if you buy something that's not a business expense or if you roll it into the next calendar year. To avoid paying taxes on UFO, either spend it on great deals for business expenses when you find them during this year, or transfer what's left into another category at the end of year. If the latter and if you transfer to a taxable category, remember to take out your profit tax rate at the time of transfer and put it in your tax savings account. For example, if you have $1000 unspent UFO and you decide to spend it on extra business debt, great! But take out the profit tax rate of, for example, 30% first and transfer the $300 to the tax savings account. Then pay the remaining $700 towards a business debt.

In the end, the percentage you should use as a profit tax rate varies by a dizzying array of factors. Your accountant will help you, because they rock. Call them today.

As a rule of thumb, be conservative. Say your profit income tax percentages yields the same 21% as the example. If 21% makes you nervous, make it 24% or whatever higher number feels comfortable to you. If you over-save for taxes, no problem. The leftover can seed your next year's tax savings account, reduce debt, be given away, or, get this, do whatever you want with it. It's your money, tax free.

Read on. Chapter 13 is dedicated to taxes.

Transferring

That's a lot of money moving around. My CAO warned me moving all this money around can cause confusion. As usual, she was right.

Here's how to keep it all straight.

1. At the end of the month, do the reconciling.
2. Once all the accounts are reconciled and reviewed, recomp the budget sheet.
3. After recomp, transfer to CERA.
4. What's left is profit.
5. Calculate and set aside income taxes.
6. Whatever is left is the net profit.
7. Split the net profit by whatever means you see fit. Both the percentage split and budget split methods will work.
8. Make transfers from the checking account directly to the separate profit split savings accounts. If using the Top Line Method of Finances, do this from your profit

savings account. If using the Bottom Line Method of Finances, do this directly from your checking account.

9. When transferring from the checking account, those transfers become entries in the checkbook register. The trail is automatically recorded in case your friendly neighborhood IRS auditor comes for a looksee.

Owner profit transfers can be made directly to your own personal accounts. There is no need for an intermediary account.

Extra business debt payments can be made directly to the lender as a check. Some banks allow debt principle payments to be made as easy electronic transfers. If writing a check, be sure to write "principle only" on the check, otherwise you may end up just pre-paying regular minimum payments. Some loans have clauses that won't allow principle only payments until a certain date.

When it comes time to spend some saved money, just transfer the amount needed back into your checking account and spend it like normal.

Owner Profit

Those owner profit transfers are pretty sweet. At home, you budget your household finances based on your salary, so when you get an influx of cash, life is good.

I have been asked what I think you should do with owner profit. This question sets me back. I think, "How should I know? It's your personal money. Do what you want with it."

Of course, I do have some thoughts on the matter.

My wife, Lisa, and I work the baby steps as we teach when coordinating a Financial Peace University class. As such, after the transfer we have a mid-month budget committee meeting, which is really just the two of us sitting down at the dining room table to adjust our budget. We add the owner profit transfer to our income at the top of our budget, and then spend it in the expense budget. In other words, we use our heads instead of our emotions. We do it as a team. We do it on purpose. It would be easy to go buy something fun which will clutter up our basement in a couple months. There's already enough stuff down there. Seriously, we need to have our own yard sale.

In lieu of stealing Dave's thunder and outlining the baby steps in this book, look them up and take an FPU class. It is perhaps the best small money you will ever spend. Honestly.

One more thing. Wherever you are in your home finances, go celebrate with just a little of the profit. Take your spouse out to eat and maybe catch a movie, or whatever you do to have cheap fun. Owner profit is a win. Rewarding yourself for the win adds motivation to go get another win!

Bacon Bits

- Figure out what your standard income tax rate is for federal and state. Call your accountant for help.
- Adjust your profit tax rate if some of your profit is spent on non-taxable items such as charitable giving or profit sharing. If this makes you nervous, skip it the first year and use the standard rate.
- Every month there is profit, multiply it by your profit tax rate and transfer the amount to your tax savings account. What's left is your net profit.
- Split your net profit into categories so you make a plan with your head and not your emotions. Use the percentage split method or the budget split method.
- Common categories could include charitable giving, owner profit, profit sharing, extra business debt payments, tank savings, and UFO.
- Keep track of transfers to and from your checking account to these savings accounts in your checkbook register.
- Celebrate!

Chapter 12: Debt

Get out and stay out.

"The borrower is slave to the lender." -Proverbs 22:7b

"Let no debt remain outstanding, except the continuing debt to love one another." -Romans 13:8a

"Rather go to bed without dinner than to rise in debt." – Benjamin Franklin

Moosehead Lake is Maine's largest lake. Dominating the Maine Highlands area, this forty-mile-long waterbody is the headwater for the mighty Kennebec River. Moosehead boasts remote villages, marinas, tourist attractions in Greenville, and some really big fish.

My grandfather took the opportunity to buy some tax-lien property back in 1953. He built a small log camp near Seboomook in a township named Big W. This camp has been my family's haven and sanctuary ever since. Much of this book was written there.

When I was a young man, many, ahem, many years ago, my father invited me for a weekend fishing trip. One beautiful morning we took the canoe out and started up a little four-horse engine mounted to a bracket. I sat in the bow while my father did the steering from the stern. We motored down along the shore and into Drummond's Cove. The salmon often run there, so we stayed and fished.

After a few hours, the wind started to pick up.

Wind on Moosehead Lake is a dangerous thing. Sometimes it causes small ripples and waves, less than a foot in height. Those are fair-weather days. Our sturdy Grumman canoe can handle it, especially with the little motor.

Sometimes, however, the wind picks up fast. It can pick up faster than a boat can get to shore. Five- and six-foot waves are not unknown on this lake. There are many boats at the bottom in testament.

We both kept watch of the wind and decided to head back toward camp. Besides, I wasn't catching any fish, which is typical for me.

As we motored back, I heard my father say something. Turning my head halfway around as only a young man can, I asked, "Did you say something?"

"It's nothing," he replied. Moments later, he said something again. With the wind in my face I couldn't make it out.

I turned again. "Huh?"

"Something's wrong. Maybe with the engine," he confessed.

"What's wrong with it?" I asked. "It sounds fine."

"I don't know. It's at full throttle now, but we're not going as fast as we should."

"Is the throttle up all the way?" As if he had not just told me so.

After fiddling with the controls for another few moments, he said, "Steering is bad, too. I've been worried about the lower unit. Maybe there's a problem."

"It seemed fine on the way here." I wasn't really adding anything to this conversation.

The canoe twisted back and forth a bit as my father continued his efforts. He finally shut the engine off. We drifted sideways with the waves, causing us to pitch and roll. He took it calmly, but I was getting nervous. But then the bow of the canoe repointed into the wind, all on its own.

"Oh!" I exclaimed. I reached over the bow of the canoe and snagged a rope tied there. I hauled up the rope hand over hand, not looking at my father. A volleyball sized rock thudded off the aluminum gunwale.

I finally looked back at him, sheepishly admitting, "Forgot to haul up the anchor."

He rolled his eyes but grinned back at me. I do this sort of thing all the time. I'd fallen into the lake that very morning. I'm known for it.

Dad restarted the engine and we were quickly on our merry way.

My father has taught me more than any man deserves to know. He has wisdom, experience, and knows more about *everything* than I ever will. His best lessons were not about any of it. The best lessons I learned many years later, when I think about the things we did together.

Debt Is an Anchor

There is an infinite combination of reasons why people go into business, but there's only one reason they stay in business. They love it.

You love your business. You love the product you provide. You love your staff and you love your customers. For those of us who love being in business, we'll never go back to just a job.

The love of business compels us to long hours and herculean effort. We operate our business at full throttle. We seize opportunities, grow the organization, and make as much profit as the market will bear. We wouldn't have it any other way.

The occasional hurdle gets our attention. When someone throws up a roadblock, we tackle it like the big man Vince Wilfork slamming into a running back. We get emotional about it. How dare they try to slow me down? Then we make our loan payments, like it's perfectly normal.

Opportunities abound. They're literally everywhere. Some of those opportunities draw on your time. Many opportunities require cash. If only we had more cash. Then we make our loan payments, like it's perfectly normal.

When we look at our slim profit margin, we spend hours innovating a way to be more efficient, sell more, and grow more. Then we make our loan payments, like it's perfectly normal.

Debt payments equal less profit.

Debt payments slow you down. You are operating your business at full throttle and debt is an anchor.

But I Needed It

I am no fan of debt, but I've had some.

I bought my business, but didn't have much cash. I make payments.

A Main-Land vehicle kicked the rusty bucket. We needed another vehicle. I hadn't saved enough money in CERA when it happened. I took out a vehicle loan.

Main-Land was growing fast. We were busting at the seams in a small office. Engineers were sitting so close they had no choice but to make actual eye contact. It was time to upgrade. I made the decision to buy instead of rent and obtained a mortgage on a building.

One winter it snowed so much and for so long, native Mainers stopped wearing shorts. Our business dropped off due to the snow and so did our cash flow. We burned through our checkbook buffer, our tank savings account, and our credit line. We had a lot of work starting as soon as the snow melted. In addition to the credit line, we had a single-payment working capital loan.

Debt is an anchor on your business. But sometimes we do it anyway.

Debt is what happens when we're not prepared. A properly funded CERA account will buy a vehicle. A fully funded saved profit account will handle an arctic winter.

I'm not going to tell you to never borrow. I try to avoid hypocrisy. I am going to tell you to become prepared so you might avoid it as much as possible.

No debt means no payments. No payments mean your budget's financial category is small. A small financial category results in a smaller expense budget section, which leads to higher profits. Remember: revenue – expenses – recomp – CERA = profit! Less expenses equals more profit. It's some kind of math.

Pay It Off

Making payments will get the debt paid off on time. Making extra debt payments will get it paid off sooner. That's why I recommended an extra business debt category in the profit budget in the previous chapter.

The order to target the debts is simple. Pay off debts with the debt snowball.

First, make minimum payments on all your debts.

Then, target the debt with the smallest balance first by meeting or exceeding the minimum payment and through profit's extra debt payment category.

Once this debt is paid off, add its minimum payment to the minimum payment of the debt with the next smallest balance. Pay it off as fast as you can with both minimum payments and your extra debt payments out of profit.

Each time you pay off a debt, the next debt's payment increases. This is the debt snowball effect. The last debt will get paid down relatively quickly using this method.

Mathematicians will want to pay off debts by smallest interest to largest interest, which is known as the debt avalanche. I'm motivated by a series of quick wins, so I prefer and recommend the debt snowball.

There are a couple exceptions. A single payment loan, often used for a short-term cash flow problem, usually requires a quick repayment when the cash arrives. Also, a credit line usually requires a paydown by a certain date. Be sure to meet those obligations.

Whichever you do, the snowball or the avalanche, tackle debt and get rid of it.

Paying debt off fast, however, requires a little motivation. There is a way to motivate yourself to increase the extra business debt payments.

Calculate and track your net worth.

Net Worth

Net worth is simply what you owe subtracted from what you own. Calculating net worth is easy math but can take some time to research all the information.

Create a chart on paper or use another spreadsheet.

On the left side, list out all the things you own and sum it at the bottom. On the right side, list out all your debts and sum it at the

Lisa and I use Google Sheets for net worth and our home budget because we can both access it anytime and anywhere.

bottom. The difference is your net worth.

Net worth is a measure of personal household wealth (you and your spouse), and also includes the value of businesses you own.

Net worth is your asset value, not the liquidation value if you were to sell everything as quickly as possible. Your car may be worth $20,000 according to Kelly Blue Book, but to sell it this month you may only get $17,000. When figuring net worth, use the $20k value figure.

Bob at Bob's Bacon Bistro calculated his net worth. This isn't my net worth, but just an example.

Asset	$	Debt	Net
Bob's Bacon Bistro	$ 564,000	$ 186,000	$ 378,000
Home	$ 180,000	$ 98,000	$ 82,000
Home Contents	$ 22,000		$ 22,000
Spouse Vehicle	$ 23,000	$ 18,542	$ 4,458
Motorcycle	$ 11,000	$ 12,500	$ (1,500)
Camper	$ 15,000	$ 8,500	$ 6,500
College ESA	$ 15,526		$ 15,526
IRA 1	$ 31,876		$ 31,876
IRA 2	$ 11,896		$ 11,896
Uncle Owen's Woodlot	$ 22,000		$ 22,000
Credit Card		$ 2313	$ (2313)
Home Checking	$ 386		$ 386
Home Emergency Fund	$ 6,543		$ 6,543
Vehicle Fund	$ 6,500		$ 6,500
Home Repair Fund	$ 3,200		$ 3,200
Christmas Club	$ 180		$ 180
Heating Fund	$ 1,680		$ 1,680
Vacation Fund	$ 350		$ 350
Total:	$ 915,137	$ 325,855	$ 589,282

Assets are listed on the left with a corresponding value. Some of those assets have associated debts.

Did you notice Bob's wife's vehicle is on the list but not his? Bob's jacked up pickup truck is owned by Bob's Bacon Bistro. Anything owned by Bob's Bacon Bistro is part of the company, including the cash assets of the business like the checking, CERA, and tank savings accounts. All the business debts are combined as the business debt.

Calculating a business value is outside the scope of my little book, but it's not hard to do. Send your email to your local SCORE branch. They routinely host business valuation seminars that will get you close enough for this exercise. Or, most larger accounting firms will have experts who can appraise your business if you're willing to pony up for an exact number.

Those funds at the bottom of the list are Bob's personal savings accounts. He uses those as sinking funds in his home budget, just like the CERA account for your business.

Bob has a net worth of $589,282. To anyone not tracking their finances, this seems pretty good! Hey, Bob is right side up!

But Bob is 50 years old. He had hoped to retire early, but he can see now he won't have enough money unless something changes soon.

Growing his business will increase its value and increase Bob's net worth. Investing more in his IRA will do the same. Increases in the stock market and real estate market will increase net worth.

Reducing debt increases net worth.

That's the point.

Figure out your net worth with your spouse. Celebrate if you are right side up. Celebrate big time if you are a millionaire! I'm talking a night at a fancy restaurant that uses tablecloths and everything!

Once the food coma wears off, track your net worth. Update it monthly. As those debts, both at home and at your business, decrease, you will be startled to see your net worth climb fast. A climbing net worth is motivation to reduce debt.

For more information on net worth, here are two great reads on the subject. *Retire Inspired* by Chris Hogan outlines net worth, investments, and retirement. *The Millionaire Next Door* by Dr. Thomas Stanley is an older but eye-opening book about what millionaires really do to increase net worth and become millionaires. Finally, go see my full booklist at www.main-landdci.com if you're interested in more options.

When is Debt Okay?

I've talked with financial experts, accountants, commercial loan executives, and CFO's. Some have used debt productively for their business, accelerating growth and accomplishing much.

Some of these experts and successful businesspeople think debt, used correctly, is a good thing. Why?

First, debt has cost in interest and fees, but lack of cash has an investment cost. There is cost either way. If the cost of debt interest is less than what the owner earns from having money, then the debt will seem a better choice. As a simple example, taking a commercial loan at 5% seems a better choice if the money is invested in your business and making 10%. In this simple example, the owner will come out 5% ahead.

Second, to get cash to avoid debt, a business owner might opt to cash in on some other equity tied up in, say, real estate or an investment. There will likely be liquidation costs.

Third, showing profit may be important. The business may be accountable to owners and shareholders who pay attention to the financial health and profitability of the company. Showing profit is one way to judge. Spending the profit in lieu of debt could result in some tough questions.

Fourth, there are significant tax incentives to debt. Assuming the debt is used to purchase a business expense, the business's tax liability will decrease. Some interest on debt is also not taxable. Intended or not, our tax code encourages borrowing.

Fifth, a large purchase may take longer than a year to save. Our tax system is not set up to let you hold those savings past December 31st. You'll get taxed on it as profit, even though you're saving for a business expense. Ouch.

Finally, and perhaps largest, there is the time of realized revenue. If the debt allows company growth which increases revenue, then the revenue will occur as soon as implemented. If the business saves for the growth for a long time instead, no increased revenue occurs over that time period. It's literally lost revenue.

I cannot find fault. This all seems true.

Yet, I still recommend limiting debt. Let me explain why.

First, risk should be factored and often is not. You'll be paying the debt back whether or not your venture succeeds. If the venture wins, you may afford the payments. If it underperforms or fails, will the payments sink you? If you save and use your own money, there are no payments either way. Don't forget to factor in your tolerance for risk, which may change with time and situation.

Next, the value of your venture may change with the market after you close on the loan. We are all at the whim of the economy. As a common example, consider real estate. Say you are a savvy real estate investor. You buy a property, and you do it with 30% down. You get a loan for 70% which you pay with the rent from the property and everything is great. But what will you do if the market tanks, your renter bails, and real estate value drops 40%? You could be upside down on the loan with no way to make payments. You remember this if you were in business in 2008.

Next, debt payments slow you down later. Once the growth has happened and you are living in a larger, presumably happier, business, the debt will be an anchor. It will slow you down. You'll wish the debt would just vanish like a teenager once the dishes are in the sink. Debt won't go away unless you make it go away, which will cost you your growth plus interest plus hurdle difficulties plus lost opportunities.

Finally, debt is stressful. When – not if – you experience a business hiccup, you may struggle to make payments. Miss a payment and you'll get a call. My personality causes me to view this as a failure on my part, and it is. Damage to company and personal reputation can result, which might lead to lost business in the future.

One more thing: your investment is way more fun when you completely own it.

If one of my kids were to own a business and asked me my thoughts about going into debt, the only business debts I might condone are a primary business building and maybe a primary business purchase if the risk of a startup is something they, like me, just couldn't stomach. Otherwise, I would suggest they save and build up to whatever they want to buy, including but not limited to: secondary businesses, investment real estate, equipment, and inventory.

There is an exception. If the purchase is so large one year of savings will not cover it, then I might borrow for some of it. For example, a woodcutter needs a skidder. I'm still trying to figure out why I need one, because skidders are awesome. But skidders are expensive. A year of business savings won't be enough. So, the interest on a skidder loan may be less than the taxes on more than one year's savings, and by a large margin. Even then, paying cash for very used and building up to something newer is recommended over debt, when feasible. Or liquidating equity (i.e. selling something) is another option. That's a judgement call you'll have to make on your own.

Many local community banks have most of their loans for the things I just mentioned above. My accounts and fading debts are at a local community bank, Franklin Savings Bank in Farmington, Maine. They are great folks who care deeply about their customers and their communities. They are just as happy to have your deposits as your mortgage and primary commercial loans. They will work with you so you can manage your money successfully. Whether or not you have debt, they want your business to prosper.

It's up to you to decide how.

Credit Lines

You probably have a line of credit. Most businesses do. If not, they've been recommended to you and you're thinking about getting one. Here's how they work.

A bank will open a new account for you with a credit limit. The limit amount depends on your business scope and credit score. This account will cost a nominal fee to set up and maintain.

As you draw on the account, usually by transferring funds to your business checking account, the available funds shrink. This continues until you reach your credit limit. You will be required to make monthly interest payments on your balance.

Does this all sound familiar? A credit card works the same way.

Some credit lines allow the loan balance to carry over year to year, just like a credit card. Many, however, have a payoff requirement. The payoff requirement typically stipulates you must have a zero balance on the credit line for at least 30 days during a twelve months period, which may be the calendar year, the date you started the credit line, or some other date range you set with your bank.

For example, if your credit line goes from September 1st to September 1st, then for 30 days during that twelve-month period you must have zero balance. If you have a zero balance from October 8th to November 8th, then you can carry a balance for the next 21+ months, from November 8th through to the following September 1st and continuing on through to the August 1st after. By then, you must have a zero balance for the remaining 30 days before September 1st. Got it? Every set twelve-month period unique to your credit line must have a 30-day period of zero balance.

Most businesses use a credit line. I do, as well. The reason is most business owners are entrepreneurs at heart. The idea of having money sitting around doing nothing just to avoid a credit line you may not use is simply anathema.

I get it. It seems a waste, right up until there's an economic downturn or some other company threat. Then, having cash on hand is suddenly invaluable, for all the reasons we discussed above concerning debt.

Because a credit line balance *is debt*.

Here's my plan. I have a credit line and will continue having a credit line, right up until I have a fully funded business emergency fund, which I build through my profit budget under the category called tank savings. Remember?

How much is a fully funded business emergency fund?

For households, FPU recommends three to six months of expenses. For your business, one to three months seems more reasonable, because the owner will have some time to adjust the business as bad times happen. That said, there is no limit. If you're conservative, save more.

If your business is growing, the amount needed in the emergency fund will be a moving target, so add more as necessary. If you're growing fast enough, you might never get there. Until you do, a credit line is your cash flow failsafe.

The Single Payment Loan

The point of this book is not to lay out all the different commercial loan products available to business owners. However, as I couldn't help but mention credit lines, I also can't help but mention the single payment loan.

The single payment loan is a one-time loan a bank will provide your business. They will transfer the amount directly into your checking account. In lieu of monthly payments to repay the loan, you will pay it back in one payment by a maturity date you agree to with the bank. This maturity date may be in a month, a few months, or more.

When you pay it back, you pay the principle and the interest for the duration you held the loan.

Most businesses use these when they have a cash flow problem. For example, you haven't been paid, but the money is coming. A single payment loan will get you through until the money comes in.

This is debt, just like any other. The thing to know about this is your repayment responsibilities. When you get paid, be sure to repay the loan. Invariably, the day you get paid some other need will crop up and the loan will take a backseat. Don't let this happen.

OPM

When I was new to business, I met a friendly man, let's call him Paul, who became a client for a significant development project. As we discussed the project and our proposal, the subject of the client's name was raised. For these kinds of things, most people form an LLC for the project. Did he plan to use an LLC? If he had one, what was its name?

"Oh, I'll have to talk to Peter about that. Peter is the money behind the project." He smiled at me because he was in with Peter, who's a solid rock in the industry.

"Peter?" I asked. "Oh, he's a great guy. I'm glad to hear you're partners in this."

"Sure," Paul assured me. "I always use guys like Peter for my projects. I learned a long time ago to use Other People's Money."

An alarm bell went off in the back of my mind, but I was too inexperienced to know why or what to do with it.

"Okay. So, should I call Peter, so he knows I'm putting his name on the proposal?"

"No, no. The proposal should be written to me. I'll give him a call tomorrow."

More alarm bells.

The project did eventually move forward, but then failed. Peter was done paying bills for Paul. Paul still owes me to this day.

OPM is an individual lender, not a bank. An individual as a lender can be dangerous if there's no collateral behind the business, whereas a bank wisely makes sure there is collateral.

Collateral risks aside, OPM can be a nefarious form of debt. The borrower may not have legal obligation to the lender. They do it specifically so they can run if they fail. They borrow from Peter to pay Paul without any skin in the game themselves. Be careful of these people. They may mean well, but my bitter experience suggests they get into trouble you don't want.

If you're going to use OPM yourself, make sure of two things.

First, do not borrow from family. I've done it. I have a very strong family and we're very close. That closeness provided many opportunities for me to worry about how my debt to them was affecting our relationship. Sometimes, the worry was well founded. Family drama is bad enough without a lender/borrower strain. Keep your debt and your family separate. Your family is worth protecting.

Second, be sure all terms of the loan or investment agreement are in writing and signed by both parties. Even if everyone could really remember what was agreed, it won't mean much in court if something goes sour. Write it all down. Sign it. Notarize it. If sizeable or anything involving real estate or expensive equipment, get an attorney's help for this.

Staying Out of Debt

Once you're out of debt, stay out of debt.

You *can* operate your business without debt, if you are prepared for it. This means a solid checkbook buffer and a full tank saving account. That's how those older, wealthy, businesspeople do it.

You haven't been financially prepared. I know this because you're reading this book. So, budget your cash flow, take some profit, and save some of it. It's how you prepare so you don't need debt.

Bacon Bits

- Use the debt snowball to pay off your debts.
- Calculate your net worth. Adjust it as you pay off debt to boost motivation.
- Recommended business debts are limited to primary business purchase and primary business real estate, if at all.
- For very large purchases, don't roll CERA to the next year. Consider building up to a bigger business by purchasing smaller and used real estate and equipment.
- Once out of debt, stay out of debt by having a good checkbook buffer and a full tank savings account.

Chapter 13: Taxes

Like death, only worse.

"The power to tax is the power to destroy." — John Marshall, Supreme Court Justice

"This is also why you pay taxes, for the authorities are God's servants, who give their full time to governing. Give to everyone what you owe them: If you owe taxes, pay taxes." - Romans 13:6-7

"We contend that for a nation to try to tax itself into prosperity is like a man standing in a bucket and trying to lift himself up by the handle." — Winston S. Churchill

I know a retired plumber who got into trouble with Uncle Sam. He did his own taxes each year and made his quarterly payments. However, he still got into trouble.

He was a shingle-hanger. He was the sole proprietor, pipe fitter, and tool carrier. His business operated out of the back of a van he parked in his driveway. His office was his dashboard, and his factory floor was his client's homes. He did great work and was beloved by family, customers, and the community at large.

The IRS saw something in his filings they didn't like. They sent him a letter, showed up at his door, and audited his paperwork. After a very stressful few months, he didn't go to jail but did get hit with a bill for $155,000.

It turns out he was guilty of multiple mistakes. Some of the mistakes were honest accounting mistakes made on the myriad of confusing IRS forms at each tax filing. Some of the mistakes involved poor or haphazard record keeping. And he may also be guilty of switching a few numbers around when he simply didn't have enough money to pay Uncle Sam.

His retirement isn't what he imagined.

Hire a Good Accountant.

Hire an accountant to be accountable for the accounting.

Lesson number one of taxes is to not do them yourself. I am an engineer and a math nerd. I deal with government authorities and regulators routinely for my work. I don't do my own taxes.

The risk of making a mistake is too high. I have never and would never cook the books, but inadvertent mistakes are possible for everyone. I make them all the time and so do you. If there is a company ending risk, you need insurance for it. Your accountant is an expert at all thing's taxes. Let them deal with the IRS.

Accountants are expensive because they're responsible professionals with expertise in an important field in high demand. They earn their money. Balking at paying their fees is natural, but mistakes can go both ways. How much money did you lose in overpayment of taxes because you didn't fully understand what was deductible and what wasn't? This may not always be the case, but it might. Lastly, you can afford an accountant because you budget for them. You do budget now, right?

Because of the large risk involved, accountants also help you sleep at night. If an IRS auditor knocks on my door, I intend to laugh, invite them in for coffee, and smile at them while I dial my accountant on the conference phone. The smile will creep them out, on purpose.

If you don't have a good accountant already, make some calls and go talk to several. You'll know a good accountant when they work hard to help you understand your tax situation. If they just tell you how much you owe with no explanation, move on. You want an accountant with the heart of a teacher.

I have an accountant who will teach me anything I want to know. I'm a little slow on the uptake, but with each passing year, I get smarter about handling my money with taxes in mind. Sometimes I call him. But if something is going on, he'll call me and let me know. He even comes to my office to sit knee to knee on occasion. Find one like him.

What Is Taxable?

This book cannot go into details on what is taxable as income and what is a legitimate business expense. I could tell you what is taxable in my business as of today, but for your business tomorrow? Sorry.

However, there are some general principles on the subject.

Much of your profit is taxable, we know. That was covered in detail back in chapter 11.

Part of your loan payments, if you have debt, is typically taxable as well. Each loan payment is partly interest, partly principle. The amount of each varies by how far into the loan schedule you are. The schedule of debt payments is called an amortization schedule. The principle part of those payments is the amortization. Each year your profit and loss statement will show total interest paid and total amortization paid. The amortization may be taxable. The interest may or may not be, depending on what your accountant tells you.

Paying for dinner with a client may or may not be taxable. The code is poorly written. Are you surprised? Those dinners add up over the course of a year, though, so be conservative and call them taxable.

There may be other taxable items as well, depending on your business. Tax code and tax case law changes as often as the IRS and businesses duke it out in court each year. Anything contributing to company growth may be taxable. Talk to your accountant about your business expense budget taxes.

Expense Budget Taxes

Back in Chapter 11 saving for income taxes on profit was discussed in detail. You have a tax savings account with money deposited every time you transfer your profits. So, tax on profits is covered. You are saving for those income taxes.

But what about the other stuff discussed above, like amortization? If there are taxable expenses in your expense budget in addition to your profit budget, then more tax savings is required if you want to keep SWAT from knocking down your door.

How much expense budget tax should be saved depends on what in your budget is taxable. Talk to your accountant and figure out how much additional money should be saved each year for those taxes. Since the expenses are only budgeted and not yet spent, this will be guesswork. Your accountant will help you get close.

If you want to figure a tax amount without your accountant, not to rely on but rather just to get an idea, then get ready for some math.

Add up all the annual expenses you think might be taxable.

Amortization is probably the big one if you have debt, as previously discussed. For now, anything contributing to company growth might be taxable, including most capital expenditures, such as company equipment or improvements to the building. Those expenses grow your business, which is taxable. But they can be depreciated, either in one year or over multiple years, depending on the equipment.

If you have any combined expenses such as your car or equipment used for both personal and business, then the personal part is also taxable. And if you buy something for personal use out of the business accounts, which I already told you not to do, that is also taxable.

See the IRS website page www.irs.gov/businesses/small-businesses-self-employed/deducting-business-expenses for more information. I'm not an accountant, so this is where you should go to learn more and keep up with changes.

Add up all those numbers to a sum of taxable annual expenses in your expense budget. Multiply it by the tax percentage, like the 30% used in the profit tax example. The result (taxable expenses multiplied by income tax rate) is the taxes owed on the taxable expenses annually. Then bump the number up a touch to be conservative.

Now you have the taxes on taxable expenses from your expense budget. Take the expense budget tax number and divide by 52. Now you know how much to transfer from your checking account into your tax savings account each week. Budget this tax expense under the financials category.

Look, there was a bunch of math there. Let's consider an example.

Bob's Bacon Bistro has the following taxable annual expenses.

Taxable Annual Expenses		30% Taxes	Weekly
Amortization	$22,000		
Capital Expense	$20,000		
Client Entertainment	$800		
Taxable Expenses Total:	$42,800	$12,840	$246.92

Client entertainment? You betcha. Bacon is a party waiting for a place to happen.

Bob's Bacon Bistro added up the amortization part of the financials budget category, all of the capital expenses, and a little bit of party marketing, for a total of $43,000 annually. Taxes on it is about $13,000. The weekly amount to save to the tax savings account is about $13,000÷52=$250. If Bob's accountant were to tell him a bunch of his capital expense could be depreciated that year, then perhaps Bob would use less of the expense in this calculation.

Why weekly? A monthly number is painfully large. Tax payments aren't something you want to miss. Transfer weekly to ease the hurt. If you are a strong budgeter, then monthly will work for you.

Because my business varies with each Nor'easter, I put my expense budget taxes on a curve. I save less for expense budget taxes in the winter and more in the summer. Consider doing so as well if your business has seasonal fluctuations.

If you end up saving too much, well, cool. This situation is discussed later in the chapter.

Salary

After getting to this point, you have a plan to make a profit from your business. About the time your business turns a profit, you need to pay yourself a salary. Exactly when is a great conversation to have with your accountant.

It is mighty tempting as the owner to pay yourself only out of profits. Whether you pay yourself through payroll or from profit, you pay income taxes either way, right? But payroll has FICA, which can be around 15%. Why would anyone pay an extra 15% on their take home money?

Because the IRS says you must.

FICA pays for Social Security, Medicare, Medicaid, and some top-secret government organizations with ray guns and sunglasses who frown on law breakers. If you skip it, you aren't paying your fair share in ray gun tax. Whether those programs are great or not is the subject of a different book I will publish right before my death at a ripe old age.

How much salary should you pay yourself? The code says you must pay yourself, and I paraphrase, commensurate with your position in your industry. If you own a three-million-dollar company, they won't accept a $20,000 annual salary. That will get you in trouble.

The good news about salary payroll is the income tax on those checks has already been paid when payroll was done. Don't save additionally to the tax savings account due to your salary.

Multiple Income Streams

Once fully into business, it can be hard for owners with an entrepreneurial bent to stop themselves from branching out into other avenues of income.

Many business owners also own the building housing their business and maybe others as well. Commonly, the ownership of the building is kept separate as a different LLC, which is smart to protect yourself from legal shinanery. Then their business pays rent to their real estate LLC. Yes, they pay rent to themselves. Rent is a business expense and not taxed to the business, but the real estate LLC rental income is taxable to the owner. Save the standard income tax percentage each month from rent income to your tax savings account. To keep the records straight, pay the full rent to the LLC, then the LLC transfers the tax savings back to the tax savings account.

Perhaps you have invested in someone else's business. When they start to return your investment, whether in payments or lump sum, save the standard income tax percentage to the tax savings account.

Maybe you wrote a book about bacon, which is selling nicely online. Again, those royalty checks are income. I'll be transferring 30% to the tax savings account, should anyone buy this book. They might, if you leave a nice review where you bought it.

Wherever your income streams come from, transfer income taxes to the tax savings account. Unless your business is a sub C-corps, your business doesn't pay the taxes. You do. Sub S-corporations and LLCs are conduit organizations which funnel all the profit to the owner. If you're a DBA (doing business as), then it's just you, the owner. All of your income is added together and taxed to you, the owner.

Other Taxes

So far, we have discussed your income tax, because it's the big one. It's so easy to get wrong and devastating when you do.

Sorry to bear the bad news, but there are other taxes. They get you coming and going.

If you own real estate, then there will likely be a property tax due once or twice a year. If you live in one of those states of nirvana with no state income tax, then your property tax is probably gargantuan.

You can save for property taxes in your tax savings account if you want. However, if your buildings are owned by a separate LLC, the LLC will likely have its own checking account. Budget separately for property taxes there. If your business pays the property taxes, budget for it in the financials category.

If you own vehicles, then your municipality will probably hit you with an excise tax each year on each vehicle your business owns. Excise is supposed to pay for maintenance on roads your company uses to do business.

Much or all of your business equipment may be taxed as a possession tax. This varies from town to town, so talk to your municipal assessor. Budget for this tax in your financials category.

There are typically two kinds of payroll tax: staff and business.

Each person on payroll must pay income and FICA taxes, including you. This is no joke. The money isn't yours; you are just paying your staff's taxes for them. Getting behind on those tax payments is like stealing from your staff. Enough said.

Meanwhile, you need to pay additional taxes to the government for the pleasure of paying your staff's taxes for them. I know it doesn't sound right, but there it is. These additional payroll taxes are paid quarterly. Don't miss them.

Depending on where you run your business, there may be other taxes as well. I wish the best of luck to my fellow Americans in New York State, the highest taxed state in the Union as of this writing.

I can't help but issue this caveat: taxes are complicated. I'm not an accountant. Even if I were, most accountants must specialize a bit just to understand their piece of the puzzle. You may be taxed in other ways for different businesses and other states. Some expenses may be taxable here but not there. Get to know your accountant. Bring them donuts. They like baked goods. And lean on their understanding.

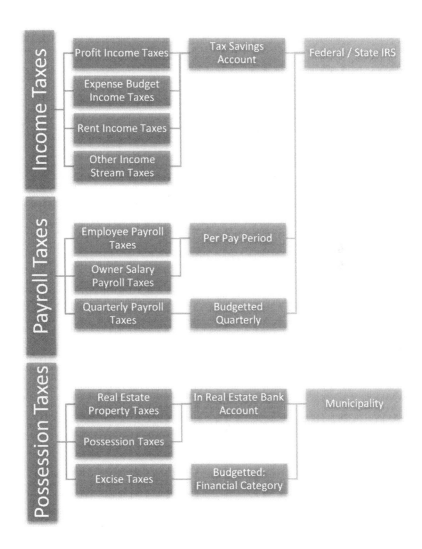

Paying Taxes

Income taxes must be paid to the state and the federal government. They must be paid in full. But they may not be paid on the government's schedule.

The government doesn't want you to pay all your taxes on April 15th. The government is supposed to operate on a budget, so it shouldn't matter if we pay our taxes once a year or quarterly. But the government isn't known for its skill at handling money. They want your tax payments spread out into four payments, known as quarterlies. Before we judge them too harshly, ask yourself, how would you like to get your salary only once a year? Yeah, it's like that.

The government wants their tax payments quarterly. There are government forms and such to figure quarterly payment amounts. Better, your accountant will calculate and provide those payment amounts, known as quarterly estimates. Then you pay those estimates on the required quarterly dates.

It sounds easy. You've been saving for taxes as you go. But, when you reach a quarterly tax payment, the amount in the tax savings account is unlikely to match the quarterly estimate. If you have a really bad quarter, you may not have much money to send at all.

If you have no money saved for taxes because of an unprofitable quarter, then don't send a payment. No profit means no or little taxes. You can't do it anyway, since you made no money and thus have no money saved for it. Move on to the following quarter. If you do have money saved in the tax savings account, which you should, then send whatever you have. If you have more than the estimate, then send the estimate and let the rest sit in your tax savings account.

Sending your tax savings account in quarterly tax payments is paying your income taxes. Then, on April 15th, your accountant does the math to see if you sent in more or less than you needed the previous year. If you sent less, you get a bill. If you sent more, you get a check back.

Sending too much is like giving the government an interest free loan. If you are saving more than the estimates, it's okay to hold some back. On April 15th, see how much they still need for the previous year and pay it.

Ideally, your quarterlies will match exactly how much is required. On April 15th, you will owe nothing and get nothing in return. This sounds great but is impractical to achieve. Owing just a little to catch up on April 15th is best. But don't owe too much, or you may not have enough saved in the tax savings account. You don't want debt with the IRS. It's a difficult balancing act and takes practice.

Another strategy is to save the money through the year and not make any quarterly payments. Just pay your taxes in one lump sum on April 15th. Then you have a stack of cash making interest for you instead of the government. I know one businessperson who does it successfully every year.

There are three problems with this strategy.

The first problem is you. The stack of cash in the tax savings account will get big. Big stacks of cash are notoriously tempting to entrepreneurs. Something will come up, whether opportunity or emergency, and you'll want to tap the account.

The second problem is radar. You don't want to be on the radar of the IRS. I know I'll be on their radar as soon as this is published, or sooner if the NSA tattles on me. It may be too late for me, but it's not too late for you.

The third problem is fees. The IRS isn't stupid. They know you would rather keep your money to the last possible moment. It's the old economic principle of the time value of money. So, they incentivize you to pay quarterly by charging you fees if you don't. Typical.

Try not to miss the quarterly dates. The dates, despite the name quarterly, aren't actually at the end of each quarter. One would think the dates would be three weeks after the end of each quarter, to give time for businesses to figure and pay their taxes. The government dates vary, instead. Put them on your calendar and pay your taxes. If you miss them, just send it in as soon as you can.

Taxes are painful. You and I both know it. But taxes are required, whether or not you think the government uses them well, whether or not you think they are too high, and whether or not you think taxation is theft. It is the law.

It sounds like I hate the government. I don't, really. I love America. I don't love impingements on freedoms or wasted tax money. Please, vote.

Fun Money

Be conservative with your tax savings.

Following the earlier examples, if 21% is the right number for profit tax savings, then use 22% or more.

If you need $250 a week for budget expense tax savings, then set it at $260 or more.

In the end, your accountant's math will dictate how much you'll actually pay in taxes. If you save more than you owe in taxes, do you know what you have? Money. You have money. Money after taxes. Tax free money.

Take the money home as a little something extra. Maybe pay down your mortgage a little, deposit it into a savings account for your kid's college, or go on vacation. Reinvest it back into your business with new equipment or expansion. Save it in your tank savings account if it's not strong enough. You can also roll it right back into your profit budget to split according to your pre-determined percentages.

If you are conservative with your tax savings, you'll have a little money left over. Call it fun money. Use it any way you want without fear of preparing for Uncle Sam.

If you want to, consider lowering your tax savings percentages and transfers to the tax savings account the following year. As you go, you will get an intuitive feel for how much to save, so follow your gut. But follow your accountant's tax savings advice more.

Bacon Bits

- Hire a good accountant who is willing to answer your questions and teach you.
- Transfer your income taxes on profit to the tax savings account, monthly. See chapter 11.
- Transfer your income taxes on taxable expenses in your budget to your tax savings account weekly.
- Transfer your income taxes on other income streams to your tax savings account as they occur.
- Pay yourself a salary. Pay your salary payroll tax with employee payroll taxes, directly to state and federal treasuries. Pay quarterly payroll taxes the same way.
- Be conservative with saving for taxes. If you over save, the money is yours, tax free.

Chapter 14: Real Priorities

Bacon is best when shared.

"Wealth is more often the result of a lifestyle of hard work, perseverance, planning, and, most of all, self-discipline." - Thomas J. Stanley

"Everything doesn't get better with money. What is bad gets worse. What is good gets better. Money is a magnifier." -Dave Ramsey

"In a sermon titled *The Use of Money,* John Wesley preached a concept that can be summarized as, 'Earn all you can, save all you can, give all you can.' That's prosperity with a purpose!" -Terry Felber

Many years ago, I knew a pair of twin sisters. Both were lovely, hardworking, and caring women. They married and started families, volunteered at church, and were well regarded in the community.

Joelle was technically older. A classic achiever, she had a great career as an attorney, specializing in family law. She made a significant salary. She both loved and hated her work with the state human services, case workers, and troubled children. Her husband, a cutting-edge chemical engineer, also brought home a strong salary.

Joelle and her husband loved to live life and have fun. They were always the life of the party! Joelle and her husband took many vacations. Their children had the newest game consoles and motorbikes. Their large house sported a three-car garage, which almost held their ski boat, kayaks, quads, motorcycles, dirt bikes, snowmobiles, and the tractor for their quarter-acre garden. They parked their shiny cars in the driveway.

They owned little of it. They may never pay off their school loans. Their home was upside down, their cars had huge monthly payments, and the credit card bill caused some hard discussions at the dining room table late in the evening.

Joelle's twin sister Trisha also loved to have fun and live life. However, Trisha and her husband decided early on to have fun within their means. Their vacations were modest and so was their home.

Trisha became a stay-at-home mom and homeschooler. She made no income but made budgeting and saving her husband's small business income a priority. Their home's mortgage was about to be paid off early, ending any debt. Their cars were used but good quality, paid for with saved money. They had no credit cards at all. They had a large emergency fund saved in the bank capable of handling half a year's expenses. They began saving for retirement the month after they were married. They also set up educational savings accounts when each kid was born so they could send them to college without student loans.

Both Joelle and Trisha were happy with their lives. Neither couple were free from stress or struggle, but they loved their families and their work.

Then one day, their father passed away while shoveling snow in his driveway. Their mother, frail for years, needed her daughters' help. This was a family emergency.

The problem was both Joelle and Trisha lived on the other side of the country from their parents. Joelle and Trisha talked on the phone and agreed to meet up later that evening for a red-eye flight. Trisha would order her ticket first, then call Joelle with the flight number.

Trisha opened up her laptop and got online to order a ticket. As usual, short notice tickets were triple the normal amount. She was about to click, "Go to Cart" when her phone rang. It was Joelle.

"Trish?" Joelle squeaked. She had clearly been crying.

"Hi Jo," Trisha said, also weepy. "I was just about to order my ticket. Flight 458. We need to be there by 7:30."

"Trish, there's a problem. I'm so sorry."

"What problem? Do you need ride?"

"No, that's not it."

Trisha's brows furrowed in concern. "Jo, what's wrong?"

"I don't…"

"Jo, you don't what? What's going on?"

"I don't have the money."

Trisha paused. She didn't have the money?

"Trish?"

"Yeah. No, that's okay, hon. I'll cover you," Trisha assured.

"I'm sorry. It's… I didn't realize. I just…"

"Jo, let's talk on the plane. Seriously, it's okay."

"No." Joelle's voice firmed after a couple of long sniffles. "It's not okay. Our cards are maxed. I hate them. We just made our mortgage payment so there's no money in the bank. I can't stand that we make so much money but can't even order plane tickets! I feel…" she trailed off. "I feel like a failure."

It was Trisha's turn to firm her voice. "Jo, now is not the time. I'll cover your ticket. Meet me there. Let's take care of mom first."

"Okay. Thank you. You're right. Of course. Thanks, little sister."

"Right." Trisha said, but Joelle heard the smile in her voice. "Do you need a ride? I think there's time to come get you."

"No. No, I'll meet you there." Joelle was back in control of herself.

As Tricia changed her order to two tickets, she said softly, "I love you. Drive safe."

What Is Money?

To be on the same page about money, we need to define it. Ayn Rand said it best. "Money … is a frozen form of productive energy." Money is some level of wealth. It isn't really paper currency, or coinage, or a number in your bank account. Money is what someone will sell you in exchange for a future purchase.

A little story about money is in order.

Imagine being a homeless hermit living in the woods of Maine. Life isn't comfortable, but the silence is wonderful.

If you were peaceably wandering the woods with a handful of berries and a partridge to your name, another hermit with no food would consider you rich. Joe is that hermit, and he wants half and asks you to share. You know you can share, and you want to share. But tomorrow, it might be you starving. So, you give Joe half of your food, but he gives you a small rock with a mark on it, which you both agree will be good for half a partridge and a few berries. Joe is a pretty good forager, so he's good for the promise. The small rock is now money.

Days later, you come upon Larry. He is also a woods hermit and currently down on his luck. Larry has no food, but he does have a new hat he found in the woods. It's blaze orange and looks warm. You like the hat. You offer the marked stone to Larry in exchange for the hat. At first Larry is dubious about a stone with a funny mark on it, but you explain Joe will give him food for it. Larry knows and trusts Joe. He makes the exchange and goes to find Joe for some food.

This is how money works. Money is an arbitrary number promising the ability to make a future purchase.

Partridge, by the way, is tasty.

Money Is Dangerous

Money is dangerous but money is not evil.

I can hear it now: but you're religious, right? A Christian? The Bible says money is, like, the root of all evil. Right?

No. Sorry. Whoever told you was wrong. People who've never read the Bible attribute much to it that's not in there.

The verse in question is 1 Timothy 6:10, which says, "For the love of money is a root of all kinds of evil. Some people, eager for money, have wandered from the faith and pierced themselves with many griefs."

Catch that? Money is not evil, but the *love of money* is the problem. Further, the love of money is only one path to evil. There are many others.

Money is not evil.

Money doesn't do a dang thing to you. It just sits there, maybe making interest or maybe stuffing your mattress and depreciating. Money won't jump up all on its own and papercut your jugular. If this happened to you, please let me know.

Instead, your own eagerness for money is the problem. The money doesn't hurt you. You hurt yourself with the love of money. The money isn't at fault. Your heart is at fault. It's a heart problem.

The Bible does have a lot to say about the evils of being rich. But the Bible also says God loves you and wants you to live a life, "to the full."

So, if being rich is evil, we need to define rich. This isn't an issue of being wealthy. If it were, then to be godly you'd have to be poorer than the poorest person in the world. Does being naked, cold, and near death in the back of the dirtiest alley sound like living a life to the full?

Is there some monetary value whereupon you become greedy? Where is the line? Remember, as soon as you have a handful of berries, you are rich compared to someone who had none.

No, money isn't evil. Money is, however, dangerous. A shot of whiskey is a problem for an alcoholic. A strip club will trip up a sex addict. My refrigerator will turn my head when there's bacon in it. And a stack of cash is temptation to the greedy.

Oh, did you just say you aren't greedy? Right. And I have no bacon problem.

We all have problems at some level with everything I just mentioned and more, including greed. One of the reasons we love money is we think it provides us security, when we should lean on God instead. Another reason is money will buy us stuff we want. We. Us. You. Me.

It's not wrong to buy stuff. Food is stuff. Shelter is stuff. Your spouse's wedding band is stuff. A vacation with your grandchildren is stuff. But is buying yourself stuff all you do with your money?

Right there is the danger with money. Having money isn't the problem. What we do to earn money isn't a problem, as long as it meets our moral code. How we spend our money is the problem because that's what drives us. The rich people we are warned about in the Bible didn't use their money as Christ would have them do.

By the way, there were rich people recorded in the Bible who used their money in righteous ways. What did the Good Samaritan do when he pulled the man out of the roadside ditch? He paid for his care, including days of stay in an inn. Nicodemus wasn't a pauper. Joseph of Arimathea had the resources to take care of Jesus' body after His death. There are many examples.

Not every rich person is evil because of their wealth, despite what you hear on the news today. Lately, it seems like so many political activists hate wealthy people, as if they did something wrong to become wealthy. Studies show very few did, and those who did got their day in the newspapers, which, of course, is all you hear about wealthy people. The sentiment today is the money making people wealthy is so wrong it's incumbent on the government to take it from the wealthy and redistribute it to everyone else. Do you see it's like a game warden taking your partridge and giving it to Joe and Larry without your consent? Anyway, that's not the point.

The point is money is dangerous. As a business owner, you'll have a lot of money flowing through your account. It'll be tempting and dangerous to your heart, your character, and your plans.

Contentment

If you follow the principles presented in this book, you are well on your way to avoiding the temptations of money. You created a budget and have a plan for the cash flow. You created a profit budget and have a plan for it. You will decrease debt to increase your net worth. You will save for taxes. Yielding to temptation means all those plans will fail. Failure is worse than death and spiders.

Once I worked my plan and I had saved up some money, the weirdest thing happened. I found contentment. I can walk into Kittery Trading Post knowing I can buy anything there, which is something many of my rural Maine friends can find only in a dream. Kittery Trading Post is awesome.

I enjoy my time with those friends, talking about this hunt or that fishing trip. Then I can happily walk out with nothing. I have found contentment with what I have. I don't need anything more.

Contentment doesn't come accidentally. Contentment occurs when you fully realize and believe your future and others are more important than new stuff. Contentment is always there for you to try, practice, and use as a tool to win.

Contentment is prioritizing your goals over your stuff.

Goal Setting

Entire books are dedicated to setting and achieving your goals. Goal setting as a subject is outside the scope of this book. However, I will give the subject a brief outline so we can talk about setting some financial goals.

Be a S.M.A.R.T.Y. with your goals.

- Specific. Make your goal specific, not vague. "I want to do better," is a great attitude, but a bad goal.
- Measurable. Make your goal with a numerical component so progress and achievement can be measured.
- Achievable. An impossible goal is a bad goal.
- Recorded. Write your goal down. If it's not in writing, it's not a good goal.
- Timed. Every good goal has a time frame and deadline.
- Yours. Someone may set goals for you, but good goals you set for yourself or adopt as your own.

Be a smarty about your goals. You might just achieve them.

Financial goals are important to winning. A well devised set of financial goals will define what financial winning is for you. Goals will provide a focus to avoid cash temptation. The end product is contentment and plan success.

I cannot and would not set your goals for you. They must be yours. But here are a few to get you started.

Make a goal to keep the budget up to date each month this year.

Make a goal to remain below budget in all your expense categories this year.

Make a goal to reach X% profit this year, and X+1% next year.

Make a goal to save a whole month of expenses in the tank savings account within two years.

Make a goal to reach a one-million-dollar net worth in five years. You'll be a millionaire!

Make a goal to reach X million dollars by age 55.

You get the idea. Set short financial goals to operate your business. Set longer term goals to save a bunch of money for emergencies, opportunities, and to help people.

Only the Strong Can Help the Weak

I was at a large retail department store a few years ago with my wife. We were Christmas shopping for our teenage boys. Our cart was piled high with Nerf guns, hunting gear, and car safety equipment.

In the next lane over, a woman started to wail.

She looked a little worse for wear. A quiet child hugged her leg, a baby squirmed in a carrier, and she had another on the way. Her clothes were a little old and her hair was out of sorts. She looked tired. Her cart was mostly full of formula and diapers, with a few toys and holiday decorations on top.

Her wail started with a gasp, then exhaled into this long, drawn-out sentence I could hardly understand. There were tears and sobs thrown in for good measure. I admit, I was scared.

Did someone step on her foot? Did she just find out she missed a sale on chocolate? Did the Patriots just lose a football game?

You already know where I'm going with this. The couple behind her paid for her cart. All of it. This woman, once under control, explained she had just left her abusive boyfriend, was living in a crowded women's shelter, and this was the last of her money. She feared for her future after Christmas. She didn't know if anyone loved her.

That couple made a real difference in her life.

They couldn't have done so if they didn't have the money.

Only the strong can help the weak. When someone is in need, only someone with the resources to spend can help them. It may be money, like the couple at the register. It may be time, like an adult helping a child with a problem. It may be a little labor, like shoveling out the older woman living alone across the street. It may be wisdom, knowledge, or possessions. Only the strong can help the weak. One must have in order to give.

Giving is the real reward for succeeding with your business finances and reason enough to follow my advice, save money, and build wealth.

When people think of the wealthy, they think of burning rolls of money in a fireplace or sleeping on a mattress stuffed with hundred-dollar bills. They think this way because they see it on television.

The reality is much different. Wealthy people give. They give great gobs of money every year to people who need their help. They give to charities. They give to individuals. They give to causes. Not because they can, but because they want to.

According to *Everyday Millionaire* by Chris Hogan, 97% of millionaires in America inherited less than one million dollars. Seventy percent didn't inherit anything. This means wealthy people in America know what life without wealth is like. That's their background. It helps explain why they give so much.

Only the strong can help the weak. Run your business finances correctly so you can build wealth and help those who need you.

There Is More to Life than Money

This book started with a simple statement. We all got into business, at some level, to make money. Of course, we did. More money means a better product, more sales, a stronger business, and wealth building.

But just like your grandmother told you, there is more to life than money. In the end, you cannot take your money with you.

As an exercise, list out your priorities in order of importance. Your priorities may differ from mine. My priorities are as follows.

1. God
2. Country
3. Wife
4. They who empty our refrigerator
5. Business
6. Community
7. Myself

In my world, God comes first. If He commands something, then I had better go do it. In fact, He's my prime priority. I will abandon all other priorities if required of me. He gave me everything, at extreme cost. I owe Him the same in return.

Next, if my country calls, I will respond. My military aged years were mostly peaceful. I never went to war, but I would have if and when called. I still would, if they accept old men who eat too much.

After the USA, my wife and my children, in that order, are my priority. Their needs are my needs. Enough said.

Then comes Main-Land. My team and their families are depending on me to provide the wages they require for their wellbeing. My clients need our services. The health of Main-Land affects many thousands of people.

Next, my community at large, as defined by me, needs my help. I will be as strong as I can to help my community as much as feasible. Volunteerism plays a large role here.

Finally, I am a priority. If my strength flags due to stress, poor sleep, and lack of exercise, then what good am I to anyone?

Logically, I cannot put all these priorities first at the same time. There are times when one suffers at the expense of another. But when push comes to shove, I choose to prioritize in this order.

Inversely, I cannot ignore any one of these priorities. Otherwise, it would not be a priority at all. Every priority needs some effort. I try to balance my effort based on these priorities but make time for all of them.

Create your own priorities and keep them someplace you can see often. Ask yourself, "Am I living according to my priorities? Are any of them out of order? Did I miss one?"

Once you have your list of priorities, review your calendar. Is your time budget out of sync with your priorities? Also, review your home budget. Is your spending budget out of sync with your priorities?

Keeping your priorities in sync with your resources will lower stress, maximize your positive impact on people, and add immeasurable joy to your life.

What Matters Most

Above, you see what my priority really is. People. Because people matter most.

At the end, when I am in the hospital ICU taking my last few breaths and choking on one last slice of bacon my favorite grandchild smuggled in for me, it's the people who will matter to me.

The money will be all given away and bequeathed to my family. I can't take it with me.

The stuff will be all be worn out, outdated, and nearly valueless.

The impact on the lives around me will continue. I hope they will in turn help others.

As a Christian, the people who are saved in part because of something I did or said will follow me to heaven. I can hardly wait for that part.

People matter most.

Only the strong can help the weak.

So, handle your finances to become strong. Then help people in need. That's the best bacon.

Bacon Bits

- Money is what someone will sell you in exchange for a future purchase.
- Money is not evil, but it is dangerous.
- Find contentment by putting your goals and others above new stuff.
- Set financial smarty goals.
- Only the strong can help the weak. Become strong to help them.

Chapter 15: Nifty Stuff
Why would anyone read this again?

"You only live once. But if you do it right, once is enough."
-Mae West

Once was enough. You don't really want to read this book again. But there may be lists, charts, or other things you want to reference as you work through your business finances.

Did you dogear a page or two? Good for you. Books are meant to be read and used, not treated like an heirloom. But for those with e-readers and those who don't deface literary marvels like this book, this section is for you.

You can also find all this information at www.main-landdci.com/buyingbacon. Feel free to print yourself off some copies of those materials, or photocopy anything from this chapter, as much as you want, regardless of all the legal speak at the front of this book. If you decide to sell it, though, I'll find you and make you fry bacon shirtless.

List of Accounts
Business
- Checking Account, your general checkbook
- Capital Expense Reserve Account, CERA Savings
- Profit Savings Account, if using the Top-Line Method
- Tank Savings Account
- Tax Savings Account
- Possession Tax Savings Account (optional)
- Profit Sharing Savings Account
- Charity Savings Account
- UFO Savings Account

Rentals / Real Estate
- Checking Account
- Property Tax Savings Account

Personal
- Checking Account
- Emergency Fund Savings Account
- Vehicle Replacement – Registration Savings Account
- College Savings Account
- Vacation Savings Account
- Property Tax Savings Account
- Heating / Cooling Savings Account
- Medical Savings Account
- Christmas Savings Account
- Home Maintenance Savings Account
- Offerings Savings Account

Steps to Budget

Revenue – Expenses – Recomp – CERA = Profit
1. Budget annual revenue.
2. Budget annual expenses.
   a. Inventory
   b. Operating Expenses
   c. Capital Expenses
   d. Capital Maintenance
   e. Marketing
   f. Financials
   g. Contingency
3. Total the annual expenses.
4. Enter a Recompensation line.
5. Budget for CERA portion of Capital Expenses.
6. Enter a Profit line, where:
   Profit = Revenue – Expenses Total – Recomp – CERA
7. If profit is too low or negative, sell more product and cut expenses.

8. If profit is above 10% or some other industry or seasonal norm, consider lowering prices to remain competitive.
9. Budget for the first month.
10. Track that month as revenue comes in and expenses go out.
11. After the month ends, reconcile the accounts.
12. Review the monthly budget.
13. If the month was in the black, hold back any recomp from previous months, if any.
14. After recomp, if the month was still in the black, transfer to CERA either the budgeted amount or revenue – expenses - recomp, whichever is less.
15. Whatever is left after revenue – expenses – recomp – CERA, is the profit for the month.
16. Apply the adjusted income tax rate to the profit and transfer it to the Tax Savings Account.
17. What is left is the Net Profit. Split the net profits.
18. Buy Bacon. I like Wrights brand bacon, but to each his own.

Our sample budget, for reference.

Bob's Bacon Bistro Budget	Annual	Jan Budget	Jan Real	Feb Budget	Feb Real
Gross Rev.	$264,000	$22,000	$18,832	$24,000	$24,981
Contracted $	$24,000	$2,000	$2,000	$2,000	$2,000
Net Revenue	$240,000	$20,000	$16,832	$22,000	$22,981
Expenses					
Inventory	$42,000	$3,500	$3,410	$3,500	$3,523
OpEx	$96,000	$8,000	$8,650	$8,600	$8,513
Cap. Exp.	$20,000	$66	$80	$50	$134
Cap. Maint.	$2,000	$167	$180	$160	$180
Marketing	$8,000	$667	$1,325	$0	$150
Financials	$36,000	$3,000	$3,000	$3,000	$3,000
Contingency	$12,000	$1,000	$632	$1,000	$462
Exp. Total:	$216,000	$16,400	$17,277	$16,310	$15,962
Recomp				$445	$445
CERA		$1,600	$0	$3,200	$3,200
Profit	$24,000	$2,000	($445)	$2,045	$3,374

We received numerous requests for a list of typical expenses that go into each of the expense categories. Remember, your categories are your choice, so split them up any way you want. But as requested, here are some ideas.

Inventory
- Department 1 Inventory
- Department 2 Inventory
- Raw Material 1
- Raw Material 2

Operational Expenses (OpEx)
- Staff Payroll: pay checks, fed & state taxes*
- Staff Bonuses*
- Quarterly Payroll Taxes*
- Retirement Contributions: both staff and company match*
- Rent
- Office Supplies
- Health Insurance: both employee and company*
- Life / Disability Insurance: both employee and company*
- Business & Liability Insurance
- Vehicle Fuel
- Heating Oil
- Utilities: power, water, sewer, internet
- Grounds: plowing, mowing, trash
- Office Services: water, coffee, cleaning
- Cell Phones*
- Professional / Society Dues
- Seminars and Training
- Consulting Services: attorney, accountant
- Employee Reimbursements
- Company Gatherings
- Building Maintenance

* Note: you may find reasons later to separate direct employee costs from other indirect business costs. It may be helpful for some businesses to separate payroll expenses from OpEx.

Capital Expenses
- Growth
- Vehicle
- Equipment
- Computer Software
- Computer Hardware
- Office Equipment Replacement
- Facility Improvements

Capital Maintenance
- Vehicle
- Equipment
- Office Equipment

Marketing
- Customer Relations
- Advertising
- Give-a-ways
- Scholarship Fund
- Golf Classics
- Graphic Arts

Financials
- Business Loan
- Bank Loan 1
- Bank Loan 2
- Credit Line Interest
- Credit Card Interest
- Credit Card Machine Payments
- Expense Budget Tax Savings
- Stockholder Expenses

Contingency

Steps to Top-Line Profit

Take your profit first, at the time of deposit:

1. Make your deposit.
2. Immediately figure profit by percentage of the deposit, from 1% to whatever is competitive in your market, during this season.
3. Immediately transfer the profit amount from the checking account to the profit account.
4. Immediately transfer the CERA amount to CERA.
5. Immediately transfer the tax percentage to the Tax Savings Account.
6. Spend the rest of the checking account using the checkbook method of finances, without a budget, you wild and crazy nut.

Steps to Profit Splitting

Split your profits. If you use the Bottom Line Method with a budget, split your profits after month end directly from your checking account. If you use the Top Line Method, split your profits after month end (or quarterly or however often you want) from your profit savings account.

The % Split Method

1. Choose categories for spending profit.
2. Use a pre-determined percentage split for each profit category. They should sum to 100%.
3. Transfer profit directly to profit accounts, your personal account, or spend, as appropriate.
4. Add up the percentages on taxable profit to apply to your standard income tax rate.

Example:

Category	%	Apply
Charitable Giving	10%	
Owner Profit	30%	30%
Profit Sharing	10%	
Extra Business Debt Payments	25%	25%
Tank Savings	15%	15%
UFO	10%	
Total:	100%	70%

The Profit Budget Method
1. Choose categories for spending profit.
2. Prioritize the categories from most to least importance.
3. Divide annual profit budget into the categories as desired.
4. Sum of annual categories must equal the annual profit budget.
5. Divide each annual category profit budget by twelve for a monthly profit budget.
6. After the end of the month, do reconciling, recomp, CERA, and adjusted income tax on profits.
7. Fund the first category as much as possible.
8. If that category was fully funded, move to the next category down and fund it.
9. Repeat step 8 until all funds are fully funded.
10. If all categories are fully funded, nice work! Go back and fund any category(s) you want with the rest.

Category	$	Monthly	Jan	Feb
Charitable Giving	$1,800	$150	$-	$300
Profit Sharing	$3,600	$300	$-	$600
Tank Savings	$3,100	$258	$-	$517
Owner Profit	$3,600	$300	$-	$600
Extra Business Debt Payments	$5,860	$488	$-	$648
UFO	$1,000	$83	$-	$-
Total:	$18,960	$1,580	$-	$2,665

Net Worth

Sample net worth chart.

Asset	$	Debt	Net
Bob's Bacon Bistro	$ 564,000	$ 186,000	$ 378,000
Home	$ 180,000	$ 98,000	$ 82,000
Home Contents	$ 22,000		$ 22,000
Spouse Vehicle	$ 23,000	$ 18,542	$ 4,458
Motorcycle	$ 11,000	$ 12,500	$ (1,500)
Camper	$ 15,000	$ 8,500	$ 6,500
College ESA	$ 15,526		$ 15,526
IRA 1	$ 31,876		$ 31,876
IRA 2	$ 11,896		$ 11,896
Uncle Owen's Woodlot	$ 22,000		$ 22,000
Credit Card		$ 2313	$ (2313)
Home Checking	$ 386		$ 386
Home Emergency Fund	$ 6,543		$ 6,543
Vehicle Fund	$ 6,500		$ 6,500
Home Repair Fund	$ 3,200		$ 3,200
Christmas Club	$ 180		$ 180
Heating Fund	$ 1,680		$ 1,680
Vacation Fund	$ 350		$ 350
Total:	$ 915,137	$ 325,855	$ 589,282

Saving for Taxes

Save for taxes for multiple taxable incomes and possessions.

1. **Profit Income Taxes.** When splitting profit, some of those categories of profit are taxable. Transfer income tax from taxable profit splits to your tax savings account.
2. **Expense Budget Income Taxes.** Some expenses are not business expenses or are not depreciable immediately. Transfer a set amount weekly to the tax savings account.
3. **Rent Income Tax.** Only if you own a building, whether you rent to someone else or to yourself, transfer taxes on rental income to the tax savings account.
4. **Other Income Stream Taxes.** Whatever other income streams come to you, transfer taxes to the tax savings account.
5. **Property Taxes.** Personal real estate property taxes are either held in escrow by a mortgage lender or saved in a personal property tax savings account. Investment properties are held by an LLC which should have its own checking and property tax savings accounts. Transfer the monthly portion of the annual property taxes to the property tax savings account.
6. **Excise Tax.** Excise tax on vehicles are due annually at registration. Budget for excise tax in the financials category and pay it out of the checking account.
7. **Possession Taxes.** This tax may be large enough to justify transfers to a possession tax savings account. Otherwise, budget for it in the financial category.
8. **Payroll.** Don't save for payroll taxes. Pay them as they come. Don't miss this important payment or your world may shrink to a five by seven cell.

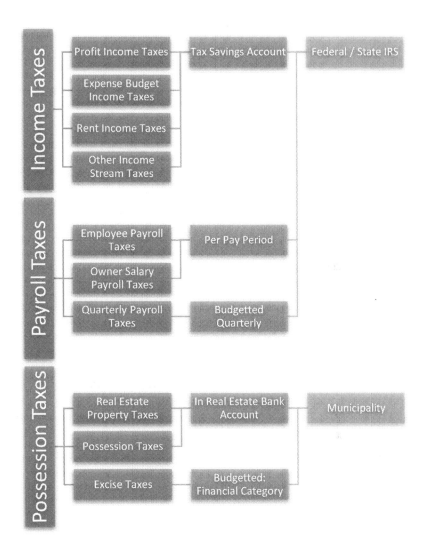

Recommended Books

These books are recommended specifically for financial learning. See the full list of recommended books at www.main-landdci.com/bobs-booklist.

Entreleadership by Dave Ramsey. If you loved Chapter 2, then this is the book for you.

Everyday Millionaire by Chris Hogan. Chris studied over 10,000 millionaires and draws conclusions.

Love Your Life, Not Theirs by Rachel Cruze. Rachel makes a case for finding contentment.

Profit First by Mike Michalowicz. This is a must-read for any free spirit wanting to try the Top Line Method of Finances. Seriously, free spirits. Read this before doing anything else with your money. Get more information at www.mikemichalowicz.com.

Retire Inspired by Chris Hogan. Retirement isn't an age, it's a number. Read this book for help on calculating and updating net worth.

The Millionaire Next Door by Dr. Thomas Stanley. This book was written in the 1990's, but still holds many truths about what millionaires do to make and keep their money. It's not what you think.

The Total Money Makeover by Dave Ramsey. The best instructional book on how to seize and maintain control of your money ever written. Period. Mic drop.

The End of Buying Bacon.

Acknowledgements

First, thank you to my friend Christine (Chris) Fournier, Administrative Director of the Jay-Livermore-Livermore Falls Chamber of Commerce for asking me to speak that morning. Lady, you got it!

Thank you to Betsy Mancine for instigating the name of this book. You are a great idea woman!

Thank you to our weekly Bible and leadership study group we call Centurions. Matthew 8:5-13. I sought to surround myself with people who thought the way I wanted to think. To your credit, gents, it's working.

Next, thank you to all my beta readers, Kendall Bliss, Jason Richard, Derek Hayes, Reverend Daren Blomerth, Pastor Henry Cooper, Matt Timberlake, and author Robin Merrill. This group of businesspeople, organizational leaders, literary gurus, and friends made me look far better than I am.

Thank you to K&J Couture Designs for the awesome cover graphics. See Kim's work at www.behance.net/kjcdesignsme.

Thank you to my Main-Landers for keeping me going. Our industry has never seen a better team, and a bossman has never been so privileged. Any day at work with you is a great day!

I thank my dad and mom for pushing me when I was young in the direction I should go. Now I'm old, and you still inspire me.

Thank you to my one and only alpha reader, my darling bride and grammar guru Lisa-Anne Berry. She was bored by the subject matter but liked the part when I called her totally awesome. It's true. She is.

Most importantly, thank you to the one and only God of heaven and earth. Jesus, there is no one who loves me more than you. Thank you for dying so I might live. Thank you for your Word. Thank you for your church and I pray she may be strong, generous, and full of love to glorify you. Come back soon. I can hardly wait.

Exhortation

This section is not something you find at the end of most books. But I am a Christian, and I just can't help it.

Not a Christian? Your eternal future depends on understanding the astounding gift provided without cost to us by our loving God Jesus Christ on the cross.

See, none of this is a cosmic accident. God made the world "very good," which is saying something from the perspective of a perfect being. But then we screwed it up by turning away from God. It wasn't just Adam. It was me, as well. And you. Think about it. We've all done bad things. Worse, compared to the holiness of God, all our sins are horrible. Even the itty-bitty things. They're all disgusting, terrible, and wicked bad compared to God's perfect holiness.

God is also a perfect judge. Would it be right for a robed judge in a court of law to free a criminal because he's the criminal's father? It wouldn't be right for God to set us free, either, not without paying the price for our crimes.

We all want into the kingdom of heaven instead of, you know, the other place. Heaven is in the presence of a perfectly holy God. He's so holy His innate glory will destroy any impurity. To get to heaven, we need to be perfect and holy as well.

Have you felt perfect lately? How about holy? Yeah, me neither.

So, it makes sense. The price must be paid for justice to prevail and for us to enter heaven. What do we need to pay? Perfect justice has only one penalty for the worst crime. Our crime comes with the death penalty.

God knows our sins. He knows every little thing we've said, done, or even thought. God knows these things because He loves us perfectly as well. He pays attention to us. He knows we don't deserve to go to heaven, yet He loves us perfectly and wants us to be with Him.

God is perfectly holy, loves perfectly, and is perfectly just. So, He did something awesome about our situation, something only He could do. Something perfectly holy, perfectly loving, and perfectly just.

He came down to earth, put on the body of a man, spent years living history's only perfect life, then paid the price for us through death on the cross. Only He could do it. And He did, because He loves us so much.

There's a catch. You're not surprised. There's always a catch. Jesus died once and thereby forgave everyone for anything they have ever done or ever will do, which only a perfect person could do. But, He will not let everyone through the gates into the kingdom of heaven. We must do our part.

Wait, what? Our part? You probably heard all this is free.

Yes, it's a gift, and what an amazing gift! But we do have a part. Our part is simple. It's also very difficult.

We must accept.

This is no light decision.

Accepting means believing. God hasn't yet scrolled back the sky and peeked through so there would be no doubt. Believing means accepting God is real even though He is invisible to us. God really did create the universe. God really did create you and I. God really did come here as a man and die for us. God really did give us a book about history and about Himself, so we could know what He wants from us.

Accepting also means submitting to His way. We Americans love to believe the illusion we are our own masters, but not so for a Christ follower. We belong to Jesus. We try to follow His way, not our way. In other words, we accept He is Lord of our lives. That's why we call Him that. We have a master and accepting means obeying.

Accepting also means being in a relationship with Him. We can believe. We can submit. But if we do not know one another, there is no relationship. This is where it gets fun. Relationship with God is awesome! He loves us, guides us, protects us, and calms us through the storms of this broken world. When I do wrong, which seems like all the time, He readily forgives when I ask and we're friends again. Just for the asking! No one in your life can match it.

There is much to gain by acceptance and so little to lose. You get knowledge, guidance, character, and joy. You get eternal life in a place of love and wonder instead of a place of fire and tears. You get to know God, with time, and be in the most important relationship of all. But before you get any of it, you must accept.

Interested? Why wait? Like my mother always said, "There's no time like the present." Accept right now. There's no magic hand gesture. There's no televangelist's number to dial. There's no password. God is with you, right now as you read this. He's knocking at your door. If you haven't already accepted Jesus as your king, then He's hoping you'll do so right now. It doesn't matter what you've done. He loves you. He's crazy about you. He wants you to know. He wants a relationship with you.

Just talk to Him. Tell Him you're sorry you messed up so bad. Ask for His forgiveness; He'll deliver it. Tell Him you want to be part of His family, a child of God. Admit to Him you cannot get into the kingdom of heaven on your own. Tell Him you'll follow Him wherever He leads and mean it.

It takes faith in Him to take this step. It's a faith that He is real. It's a faith His way is better than your way. It's a faith His promises are true.

But it's not a blind faith. Read about His way in the bible. Try the book of John. Try the book of Romans. Try any of it, because His love has been steady throughout history.

Want to know more? Go to www.fayettebaptistchurch.org. If you've just accepted, email them and ask for more information. Someone there will reach out to you and help you find someone in your area who will walk with you on your journey with God.

About the Author

Robert (Bob) L. Berry III, P.E. is a country boy from the back woods of Maine. Whenever he can, he escapes to some quiet corner to the north, usually upta camp on Moosehead Lake, to fish poorly and chase wood's critters with a bow and arrow.

Bob owns and runs Main-Land Development Consultants, Inc., a land consulting firm of engineers, surveyors, and environmental scientists helping people build economies and support communities all over Maine and beyond.

Bob serves on the board of directors for the Franklin County Chamber of Commerce, the Greater Franklin Development Council, New England Bible College, and Mt. Blue TV. Bob helps on the committees for the annual Apple Pumpkin Festival in Livermore Falls, the annual Business Expo in Farmington, and the annual Spruce Mountain Sled-In Winter Festival in Jay, the latter of which he founded in a rash moment of overexuberance.

Bob also serves on the board of directors for Franklin Savings Bank, based in Farmington, Maine. Bank with Frank!

Bob wrangles middle schoolers in the Fayette Baptist Church youth program, Ignite, and at Sunday school. Matthew 5:16. Shine on, you amazing kids! Shine on!

Bob lives in Jay, Maine, with his wife Lisa, who is also an author, three sons: Benjamin, Nathaniel, and Jackson, all of whom he is extremely proud, and his wife's rotund, nefarious cat named Maggie, but whom he calls Meatloaf. Bob's pretty sure it's plotting to kill him.

Made in the USA
Middletown, DE
14 February 2020

84342596R00106